THE
Amazing Mom Book

THE
Amazing Mom Book

*Real Facts, Tender Tales,
and Thoughts from the Heart
About the Most Important
Person on Earth*

JOHN MACINTYRE

SOURCEBOOKS, INC.
NAPERVILLE, ILLINOIS

Published by Sourcebooks, Inc.
P.O. Box 4410, Naperville, Illinois 60567-4410
(630) 961-3900
FAX: (630) 961-2168
www.sourcebooks.com

ISBN 1-4022-0355-1

Library of Congress Cataloging-in-Publication Data

MacIntyre, John
The amazing mom book / John MacIntyre.
p. cm.
ISBN 1-4022-0355-1 (alk. paper)
1. Mothers. 2. Motherhood. I. Title.

HQ759.M299 2005
306.874'3--dc22

2004029624

Printed and bound in Canada
WC 10 9 8 7 6 5 4 3 2

Dedication

*Anybody writing a book about mothers
had better take the opportunity to thank their own mother.
In my case, there are two mothers:
Lynn, who nurtured me and nine other offspring;
then, of course, there is my wife, who is also a mother.
Together they have made my life richer and worth
living in so many different ways.*

Table of Contents

Introduction 1

Mother's Day: Then and Now 3

And So It Begins...Baby Comes Home 13

Motherhood through the Ages 30

The "Second Oldest Profession": Moms Raising Kids 50

Moms at Work 62

Moms Across Cultures 71

Mothers of the Earth 86

Mothers on Screen, Stage, Page, and Canvas 99

Moms of the Animal World 131

Thanks, Mom 145

Medical Mom 156

Royal Moms 168

Mothers in Law 187

Brains, Brawn, Beauty, and Bravery: Moms with
 Extraordinary Talent and Conviction 203

Mom @ Home 223

Mythological Mom 251

Acknowledgments

I owe a large debt to my dedicated researcher, Martha Walls-Slumkoski. We have worked together for eight years, through deaths in families, snowstorms, and now, in Martha's case, a PhD. To call Martha a researcher is perhaps inaccurate, because I see her handiwork all over the final manuscript and any other work that I've done. I would also like to thank Nick Hatt who also pitched in on the research. Additionally, I would also like to thank my agent, John Willig, for staying the course, and my family for always being there. Cheers.

Introduction

We all have a mother. She sees in us all that we are and all that we are capable of being. She is our greatest champion. When the television cameras pan the sidelines of an NFL game, or peek into the dugout of a baseball game, you see huge men saying two words: "Hi, mom." What they are saying, of course, is look at me, but also look what you have made of me. Look what we've made together.

Our mother has seen us through runny noses and fad haircuts and she still declares us beautiful. She knows we flunked chemistry (three years running) and still assures us of our brilliance. Where we see our failings, mom sees only our boundless potential.

She clothes us, feeds us, burps us, nurtures, and teaches us. She is there when we are frightened or when we fall. Mature adulthood, especially parenthood, gives us all a new appreciation of our mother and motherhood. All of a sudden we realize that the "mom-isms" that all moms spout for the first decades of their children's lives are not merely meaningless motherhood mottos—they are true. As it turns out they weren't designed to annoy, but to protect us, educate us, and help us become better, happier people.

Mom's indelible imprint shapes the adults and parents we become. This book is meant to celebrate you, mom. It recognizes your sacrifices, demonstrates your devotion, and is in awe of your love.

Mom, you have not only shaped who we've become, you have shaped the world we live in. It should come as no surprise that we dedicate this book to the most important mom of all—you!

Mother's Day: Then and Now

"God bless our faithful good mothers."
—Anna Jarvis, founder of Mother's Day

Ancient Mothers

Days to celebrate maternity and the mothers among us date back to ancient times:

- The Greeks honored Rhea, mother of gods and goddesses, with an annual springtime festival.

- Hilaria, an ancient Roman holiday, paid homage to the mother goddess Cybele.

- In the middle ages, motherhood was celebrated among European Christians through the mother Mary.

- In Britain of the 1600s, mothers received more secular adoration when "Mothering Sunday" was set aside as a day that servants could be excused from their toil and freed to visit their mothers. To mark the occasion and to show their affection and respect, those who could afford it presented their mother with a "mothering cake."

Although rooted in these centuries-old traditions, Mother's Day celebrations as we know them today only began in the late 1800s.

Mother's Day in America

In 1872, American Julia Ward Howe, a pacifist, suffragist, and author of "The Battle Hymn of the Republic", suggested that a day dedicated to peace be established in the United States.

America had been ravaged by the Civil War, and Howe was deeply moved by the war's horrendous effects. Howe's quest for a day dedicated to peace was directed toward the mothers of the nation. In her "Mother's Day Proclamation," clearly imbued with her feeling as a mother and her anti-war sentiments, Howe pleaded:

Arise then…women of this day!
Arise, all women who have hearts!
Whether your baptism be of water or tears!
Say firmly:
'We will not have questions answered by irrelevant agencies,
Our husbands were not come to us, reeking with carnage,
For caresses and applause.
Our sons shall not be taken from us to unlearn
All that we have been able to teach them of charity, mercy
*   and patience.*
We, the women of one country,
Will be too tender of those of another country
To allow our sons to be trained to injure theirs.'

Following Howe's lead, in 1907, Philadelphia native Anna Jarvis wished to establish a day of recognition for women and mothers. The focus of the day envisioned by Jarvis was to set aside a day to honor mothers, especially their contributions to peace and worker safety.

National Recognition

Jarvis did just that in 1910 when she held a celebration to honor her own late mother. In 1910, West Virginia was the first American state to acknowledge Mother's Day, and by 1911 most states had set aside the second Sunday of May to pay homage to moms. In 1914, President Woodrow Wilson proclaimed Mother's Day a national holiday with the following proclamation:

Whereas the service rendered the United States by the American mother is the greatest source of the country's strength and admiration; and Whereas we honor ourselves and the mothers of America when we do anything to give emphasis to the home; and Whereas the American mother is doing so much good for government and humanity; we declare that the second Sunday of May will henceforth be celebrated as Mother's Day.

A movement originally designed to celebrate the role of women in the peace movement and in improving workplace conditions evolved into a holiday to recognize motherhood in a more general sense.

Mother's Day Today

- Americans spend $10.5 billion on Mother's Day annually.
- According to a survey by The UPS Store and Mail Boxes Etc., 74 percent of Americans will buy at least one Mother's Day gift this year.
- Nine in ten Americans honor mom in some way.

Din Din

- According to the National Retail Association, 36 percent of Americans take mom out to dinner to celebrate her day.
- Seventeen percent outfit mom in new clothes.

You've Got Mail

- American households send one hundred fifty million Mother's Day cards annually.
- Hallmark makes fifteen hundred different Mother's Day cards.

"It's For You."

- According to an AT&T survey, American moms receive 122.5 million phone calls in America on their special day from grateful kids everywhere.

- Sixty-eight percent of American kids call their mom on Mother's Day.

- Three percent calling mom will call her collect.

Momma's Boy

- On average, men spend $86.10 on Mother's Day, while women spend $60.80, according to the International Mass Retail Association.

- Sons are more likely to treat mom to flowers on her day. Forty-nine percent of men buy moms flowers, while 46 percent of women do the same for their mom.

- Sons are also more inclined to take their moms out to brunch. While 47.7 percent of men take mom out for brunch, just 29 percent of women do the same.

Mother's Day: A Global Perspective

Mothers are celebrated in virtually all cultures around the world, and most have a special day set aside for their celebration. Many nations celebrate Mother's Day with the U.S. on the second Sunday in May. These include: Australia, Belgium, Canada, Denmark, Finland, Italy, Japan, and Turkey.

Other nations have a fixed date of May 10 to celebrate moms each year: Bahrain, Hong Kong, India, Malaysia, Mexico, Oman, Pakistan, Qatar, Saudi Arabia, Singapore, and United Arab Emirates are among those who pay homage to mom on May 10.

Some other dates for Mother's Day around the world are:

- Argentina on the second Sunday in October;

- France on the last Sunday in May;
- Lebanon on the first day of Spring;
- Norway on the second Sunday in February;
- South Africa on the first Sunday in May;
- Spain and Portugal on December 8;
- Sweden on the last Sunday in May. ❦

❦

Rainy Day

Ethiopia has no set date for Antrosht, that nation's Mother's Day. Instead, a holiday that celebrates mothers happens whenever the rainy season ends. In a two- or three-day festival, children come from all over to visit parents. They bring the ingredients for a traditional meat hash, which is prepared by their mother. Mothers and girls anoint themselves with butter, and whole families sing songs celebrating family and tribal heroes.

Tie Up the Children

Mother's Day in Yugoslavia is part of a three-part holiday. It commences on a Sunday in early December with Dechiyi Dan, or Children's Day. On this day, parents tie up their children and refuse to release them until they are good. Materice or Mother's Day is celebrated the next Sunday. On this day, children tie up their mother, and release her only when she has provided sweets or other goodies. The third Sunday celebrates Ocevi, Father's Day. Children tie their father to a chair or bed. To win his release, father must promise more expensive gift items—and these appear as Christmas gifts some days later.

World Views That Honor Mom

Around the world, motherhood is an esteemed, sacred identity:

- Some tribes, such as the Assam people of Africa, refer to themselves not as families, but as maharis, or motherhoods.

- In China, family names often begin with a sign that means "mother"—this is a way to pay homage to their female ancestors.

- Japan's Imperial Family traces its descent from Omikami Amaterasu, the Mother of the World.

- In North America, Native American women have long been honored with the name "Life of the Nation" in recognition of their gift of motherhood to the tribes.

Statistically Speaking

Scientifically speaking, May might just be the best month for Mother's Day. Babies born in May are, on average, two hundred grams heavier than those born in any other month.

MARY, MOTHER OF...

Little is known of the personal life of the Virgin Mary, mother of Jesus Christ. Her father, Joachim, was allegedly descended from the royal family of David, while her mother, Anna, was said to be descended from the priestly family of Aaron.

In childhood, Mary was presented at the local temple for recognition and education, a tradition typically reserved for Jewish sons. As a youth, she was engaged to Joseph, and visited by an angel who informed her that although she had never known the physical act of love, she would give birth to the Son of God.

Once Jesus set about his work, Mary did not interfere. It is said, however, that Mary watched her son attentively, observing and learning from his divine message. Mary was present at the time of her son's crucifixion, and met Jesus as he labored to carry his cross to Golgotha.

Mary attended to her son as he suffered long on the cross, and her devotion to her son at his moment of trial made her a mother figure for all Christians. Mary remained an important figure in the fledgling Christian church, which believed that upon her death she, like her son, ascended to heaven, physically and spiritually.

Catholics continue to pray to Mary as an alternative channel to God's ear and Protestant sects look toward Mary as an embodiment of supreme faith. Nobody would deny that she was important to the life and message of Jesus Christ.

Take Five: Top Five Best Gifts for Mother's Day

1. Handmade gifts
2. Jewelry
3. Flowers
4. Spa/pampering
5. Get-away trip

Take Five: Top Five Worst Gifts for Mother's Day

1. Nothing
2. Household appliances
3. Cooking/cleaning supplies
4. Socks
5. Non-fitting clothes

Source: Wishlist Inc.

Mother's Day in Bloom

Flowers have long been associated with Mother's Day. In its early days, Mother's Day in the United States was marked by special church services at which worshippers wore white carnations to honor living mothers, and red carnations to remember moms who had passed away. Although this tradition has fallen by the wayside, flowers continue to be an important part of the holiday.

May is a busy month for America's 23,870 florists and the 125,116 people who work in the industry. More people purchase fresh flowers and plants for Mother's Day than for any other holiday except Christmas.

- According to the National Retail Association, 23 percent of all holiday sales of flowers and plants are accounted for by Mother's Day.

- Thirty-three percent of all Americans will buy mom flowers for Mother's Day.

- Eight percent of moms love flowers so much they buy them for themselves!

How Do You Like Them?

Each May, mothers are treated to a variety of floral gifts, according to the American Floral Endowment's Consumer Tracking Study.

- Thirty-seven percent of moms receive outdoor bedding and garden plants.

- Twenty-two percent receive flowering and green plants.

Sweet Smell

By giving the gift of flowers, kids make their moms happy. A recent Rutgers behavioral study has demonstrated that "not only do flowers make us happier than we know, they have strong positive effects on our emotional well-being."

Take Five: Top Five Types of Cut Flowers Given for Mother's Day

1. Mixed flowers
2. Roses
3. Carnations
4. Daffodils, irises, tulips
5. Chrysanthemums, daisies, lilies and orchids

Source: American Floral Endowment's Consumer Tracking Study.

Deep Blue

On Mother's Day 1997, IBM's computer, "Deep Blue," the "mother" of all computers, defeated world chess champion Garry Kasparov— marking the first time a machine beat a world chess champion.

Great Expectations

- Just 1 percent of mothers polled by Gallup say that they do not expect to receive a Mother's Day gift from ungrateful offspring.

- Of those with more considerate children, 37 percent expect to receive a card, 35 percent expect to be taken out to dinner and 28 percent expect a phone call from dutiful kids.

- Seventeen percent expect a handmade gift and 17 percent expect flowers.

- Two percent are fence sitters, unsure as to whether or not they will receive a Mother's Day gift.

*"Mother was one of those strong, restful, yet widely sympathetic
natures, in whom all around seemed to find comfort and repose."*
—Harriet Beecher Stowe

HARRIET BEECHER STOWE

Harriet Beecher was born in 1811, the seventh of eleven children of Rev. Lyman Beecher, a prominent Protestant minister, and Roxanna Foote Beecher. Although her mother died when Harriet was just five, she imparted to her daughter a life-long love of learning. Harriet was an avid student and eventually became a teacher herself at the Hartford Female Seminary.

As a teacher, Harriet impressed the skill of writing on her students. In 1836, Harriet married a widower and professor, Calvin E. Stowe. Harriet Stowe was soon to find fame as a writer herself. Initially writing to supplement her family's income, her talent brought her national fame when she published *Uncle Tom's Cabin* in 1852. A then controversial work, Stowe's novel was a powerful antislavery book that humanized the terrible plight of slaves in America and rallied abolitionist forces in the United States.

A CLASSIC

Although Stowe is known for her powerful writing (her book has never gone out of print), she was also a devoted mother to seven children: three daughters and four sons. Her experiences as a mother were often recounted in her writings. For example, her fear that her oldest daughters, twins Eliza and Harriet, were becoming too frivolous contributed to her characterization of young women in *My Wife and I* and *We and Our Neighbors*.

Similarly, her son Frederick's battle with alcoholism inspired the character of Tom Bolton in both these books. Finally, the pain she experienced when her oldest son Henry drowned at the age of nineteen was recounted in *The Minister's Wooing*. Stowe was extraordinarily proud of her motherhood and once wrote: "My children I would not change for all the ease, leisure, and pleasure that I could have without them. They are money on interest whose value will be constantly increasing."

2

And So It Begins...
Baby Comes Home

"Making the decision to have a child—it's momentous.
It is to decide forever to have your heart go walking around
outside your body." —Elizabeth Stone

Getting Started

- A woman becomes pregnant most easily at the age of eighteen or nineteen, with little real change until the mid-twenties.

- There is then a slow decline to age thirty-five, a sharper decline to age forty-five and a very rapid decline as the women nears menopause.

Did You Know...

- That during pregnancy, the uterus expands to five hundred times its normal size?

- That a woman's arthritic pains will almost always disappear as soon as she becomes pregnant?

- That "small people" almost always have full-sized children, even if both parents are "small people"? ❦

Quotable Mom

"The mother's heart is the child's schoolroom." —Henry Ward Beecher, preacher, orator, lecturer, writer, editor, and reformer

"If I had my life to live over, instead of wishing away nine months of pregnancy, I'd have cherished every moment and realized that the wonderment growing inside me was the only chance in life to assist God in a miracle." —Erma Bombeck

❦

He's With Child, Too

If you've found your husband or significant other acting out your pregnancy, then there is a very real possibility he might be suffering from Couvade Syndrome. Couvade is a phenomenon where an expectant father experiences some of the same bodily symptoms during pregnancy as his pregnant partner. The word "couvade" is derived from the French word *couvee*, meaning "to hatch," and really hatching or giving birth (you, not him) is usually the cure for the syndrome.

Couvade's symptoms often include indigestion, increased or decreased appetite, weight gain, diarrhea or constipation, headaches, and toothaches. Onset is usually during the third gestational month, with a secondary rise in the late third ❦ trimester.

Couvade has been seen as an expression of bodily anxiety, pseudo-sibling rivalry, identification with the fetus, ambivalence about fatherhood, and as a statement of paternity. Others have seen it as the psychosomatic equivalent of primitive rituals of initiation into paternity. The occurrence of Couvade's symptoms by expectant fathers has been reported to exist in American and European males.

There have also been doubters in the medical community. Doubters say that the symptoms expectant fathers display may be caused by the changing eating habits of the mother, nerves, or other changes brought about by the pregnancy. Whatever the case, be good to him, because he's going through pregnancy, too.

Quotable Mom

"Giving birth is little more than a set of muscular contractions granting passage of a child. Then the mother is born."
—*Erma Bombeck, comedian & author*

Take Five: Five Home Remedies for Morning Sickness

1. Ginger
2. Potato chips
3. Crackers
4. Almonds
5. Lemons or lemonade

Mom's Eyes

- According to a study of genes, left-handed mothers are more likely than left-handed fathers to produce left-handed children.

- A theory spreading through the scientific community suggests that the time of your child's birth sets his or her physical clock. According to the theory, if your child was born around dawn, he or she is more likely to be a "morning person" and do his or her best work at that time of the day. If he or she was born in the late afternoon, he or she is not expected to perk up until the evening.

- A survey conducted at Iowa State College suggests that a parent's stress at the time of conception plays a major role in determining a baby's sex. The child tends to be the same sex as the parent who is under less stress.

- According to the ancient Greek philosopher, Aristotle, it is wind direction that determined whether a baby would be a boy or a girl.

Babies in America

- According to census information, four million American moms give birth every year.

- Forty percent of births are mom's first baby, 33 percent are a second-born, 17 percent are a third child, and 11 percent of births are baby number four or more.

- Although the vast majority of American births now take place in hospital, 36,000 of births were attended by doctors or mid-wives in a non-hospital setting.

August Is For

- According to census information, the most prolific baby-month is August.

- And then there is something about Tuesdays: more babies are born on Tuesdays than on any other day of the week.

- Today, the average age at which moms first give birth is 24.8.

- Increasingly, women are delaying motherhood. In 1980, 2 percent of new moms were in their forties; that figure has jumped by 50 percent in the last twenty years..

Journey to Life

Sperm meets egg within the fallopian tube and the miracle of life begins. Although several sperm may penetrate the egg's outer layer, only one sperm will enter the ovum and fertilize it. In the middle of the ovum, the chromosomes of mother and father splash about and bits of information from both begin to form the chromosomes of the baby. At the moment of conception, the baby's gender is determined thanks to the sex chromosomes in the father's sperm.

MONTH ONE

The blastocyst or sprout pouch makes its way to the uterus, searching for a spot to settle. Cells divide into two groups—those that form the placenta and those that form the baby. The blastocyst burrows itself into the lining of the uterus, a process called implantation.

MONTH TWO

Elbows have started to form and arms and fingers have begun to develop. Leg buds begin to show feet with tiny notches for toes. The face continues to change as the ears, eyes and the tip of the nose appear. The intestines start to form in the umbilical cord. Teeth develop under the gums and there should be a fluttering heartbeat.

At the end of the second month of pregnancy, the baby looks like a tiny human infant. If it is a boy, the penis will begin to appear. The baby is a little over one inch long and still weighs less than one ounce.

MONTH THREE

Almost all of the organs and structures of the fetus are formed. Fingers and toes have separated and hair and nails begin to grow. The genitals begin to take on their gender characteristics.

Amniotic fluid begins to accumulate as the baby's kidneys begin to produce and excrete urine. The muscles in the intestinal walls begin to practice peristalsis—contractions within the intestines that digest food.

The baby will be completely formed by the end of the month and may have begun moving its hands, legs, and head, and opening and closing its mouth. The baby's heart has four chambers and beats at 120 to 160 beats per minute.

MONTH FOUR

The baby's skin is pink and somewhat transparent. Eyebrows and eyelashes begin to appear. Buds on the side of the head begin to form into the outer ear. The head makes up about half of the baby's size and the baby's neck is long enough to lift the head from the body.

The baby moves, kicks, sleeps, wakes, swallows, and passes urine. Mothers may start to feel a slight sensation in the lower abdomen (called quickening). This feels like bubbles or fluttering. By the end of the month, the baby will be eight to ten inches long and weigh about six ounces.

MONTH FIVE

This is a period of tremendous growth for the baby. Internal organs are maturing. Fat is being stored beneath the baby's skin. The baby is growing muscle, and blood cells take over for the liver the job of producing blood. The baby's gall bladder will become functional, producing bile that is necessary for digestion. The baby sleeps and wakes at regular intervals and turns from side to side and head over heels. At the end of the fifth month, a baby will be about ten to twelve inches long and will weigh about one pound.

MONTH SIX

The baby's brain is developing rapidly. Fatty sheaths, which transmit electrical impulses along nerves, are forming. Meconium, the baby's first stool, is developing. A special type of fat (brown fat) that keeps your baby warm at birth is forming. Baby girls will develop eggs in their ovaries during this month. Bones are becoming solid. By the end of the sixth month, the baby will be around eleven to fourteen inches long and will weigh about one to one-and-a-half pounds.

MONTH SEVEN

The baby's eyes can now open and close and sense light changes. He or she can now hear the outside world quite well over the sound of your heartbeat. The baby exercises by kicking and stretching. He or she can also make grasping motions and likes to suck its thumb. The baby will be about fifteen inches long and weigh about two or two-and-a-half pounds by the end of this month.

MONTH EIGHT

Bones are getting stronger, limbs are fatter. The brain is now forming its different regions and it, along with the nerves, direct bodily functions. The baby may now hiccup, and has the ability to taste. All five senses are functional. A boy's testicles will have dropped from his abdomen where they will then descend into his scrotum. The baby is up to four pounds now.

MONTH NINE

The baby is now gaining a half pound each week. The baby is settling into the fetal position with its head down against the birth canal, its legs tucked up to its chest, and its knees against its nose.

The mother's antibodies to disease begin to flow rapidly through the placenta. Fifteen percent of the body is fat and the chest sticks out. The baby is now about twenty inches long and weighs approximately six to nine pounds. The baby may be born anytime between the thirty-seventh and forty-second week of pregnancy.

Quotable Mom

"The commonest fallacy among women is that simply having children makes one a mother, which is as absurd as believing that having a piano makes one a musician."
—Sydney J. Harris, author and journalist

Putting A Price on It

Aside from medical costs, it has been determined that new parents in the U.S. typically spend $7,000 dollars in a baby's first year on everything from diapers to formula to daycare, according to allaboutmoms.com.

Amazing Baby Facts

- A fetus in the womb can hear.
- A fetus will respond to sound and to bright light shone on the mother's belly.
- A newborn baby's head accounts for about one-quarter of its entire weight.
- Babies prefer "pretty" faces to "plain" ones, according to researchers at the University of Texas.
- Babies are born with 300 bones, but by adulthood humans have only 206 bones in the body. Various bones fuse together during the maturation process.

Sad Facts

- Overall, the infant mortality rate of American babies today (per 1000 live births) is 6.8, according to the Bureau of the Census.

- Delaware has the highest rate, at 10.7, and New Hampshire the lowest, at 3.8.
- On the plus side, the infant mortality rate has improved dramatically over the past four decades. In 1960, the rate was twenty-six per one thousand live births.

Birth Then and Now

- On average, American moms now have two children, according to the Bureau of the Census—a far cry from seventeenth century America, when moms had thirteen children.

- The number of triplets born in the U.S. today is more than triple the number born in 1971, an increase attributed to older age of mothers and the use of fertility drugs.

- In 1970, 10.7 percent of births in the U.S. were to unmarried moms. Today, 33.5 percent of all births are to unmarried moms.

- In 1985, 39,000 American births did not take place in the hospital. Today, this has fallen to 26,000.

Mikey

One birth fact has remained pretty constant—American parents are as enamored with the name "Michael" as much today as they were fifty years ago. Mike consistently makes the top ten in most popular names. In both 1999 and 1950, Michael topped the list of favored boy's names.

Did You Know...?

- Somewhere in the world a baby is born every three seconds and in America a baby is born every eight seconds.

- In the vast majority of the world's languages, the word for "mother" begins with the letter M.

- Missy is the name of Snoopy's mother in the Peanuts cartoon strip.

- The first woman to give birth in an airplane was Mrs. T.W. Evans, on October 28,1929, over Miami.

- The first child ever born on the continent of Antarctica arrived in 1978.

- The first woman to give birth in the White House was Martha Randolf, daughter of President Thomas Jefferson, on January 17, 1806.

- The oldest verified mother was Mrs. Ruth Alice Kistler of Portland, Oregon. She was fifty-seven years, 129 days old.

- The youngest woman to learn that she was a great-great-great-grandparent was Mrs. Ann V. Weirick (1888-1978) of Paxtonville, Pennsylvania at the age of eighty-eight.

Quotable Mom

"In the sheltered simplicity of the first days after a baby is born, one sees again the magical closed circle. The miraculous sense of two people existing only for each other."
—Anne Morrow Lindbergh

"When a child enters the world through you, it alters everything on a psychic, psychological and purely practical level."
—Jane Fonda

Mother's Little Helper

A five-year-old boy helped to deliver his baby sister after his mother unexpectedly went into labor in the bathroom of their home. Connor Young, from Irvine, Ayrshire, ran upstairs after hearing his twenty-six-year-old mother, Debbie, screaming. She gave birth within minutes of collapsing with contractions.

Connor talked to her and kept her conscious as he untangled the umbilical cord from around the baby's neck. He then wrapped the 7 lb.12 oz. baby in towels to keep her warm before telephoning his grandmother for help and announcing: "Mummy's having a baby in the toilet." Paramedics were called and arrived on the scene within minutes. They found Connor comforting his shocked but happy mother and his new baby sister, Courtney, in the bathroom.

The baby was in perfect health. The family was taken to Ayrshire Central Hospital in Irvine, where Ms. Young and Courtney stayed for a few days to recover. Connor, who has epilepsy, was sent to stay with his grandmother. Ms. Young said she could not have coped without her "little star."

Take Five: Top Five Baby Names for Girls

1. Emily
2. Madison
3. Hannah
4. Emma
5. Alexis

Take Five: Top Five Baby Names for Boys

1. Jacob
2. Michael
3. Joshua
4. Matthew
5. Ethan

Source: Statistical Abstracts of the U.S.

You Just Know They'll Be Teased

There are two American babies named ESPN, in honor of the sports channel. Seven boys are named Del Monte, 49 boys named Canon, six boys named Timberland, and 300 girls named Armani.

Names With Great Mileage

In America there are twenty-two girls named Infiniti, five named Celica and fifty-five boys named Chevy.

Sleep On It

- In 1994, the U.S. National Institute of Child Health and Human Development launched its "Back to Sleep" campaign—a campaign encouraging parents to have babies sleep on their backs.

- The campaign has been a resounding success; between 1992 and 2003, the number of babies who died of Sudden Infant Death Syndrome was reduced by 50 percent.

A Massage, Please...

- Parents in India, China, and South America have long recognized the value of infant massage, a practice that is growing in the United States.

- The number of trained infant massage instructors in America soared from twenty-five hundred in 1998 to almost six thousand in 2003.

Adoption in America

- According to the Bureau of the Census, approximately one million children in the United States live with an adoptive parent.

In 1992 alone, 127,441 children were adopted in the United States.

- Forty-two percent of adoptions were by a stepparent or other relative.
- Fifteen-and-a-half percent were adopted from foster care, and 5 percent were adopted from other countries.
- In 2002, Americans adopted 5,053 children from China, 4,939 from Russia and 2,219 from Guatemala.

A Mother's Intuition

Seventy percent of blind-folded mothers who spend at least one hour with their newborns can choose their infant from a group of three just by the feel of the backs of their hands, according to the journal, *Developmental Psychology*.

Multiplicity

- According to the National Center for Health Statistics and the U.S. Department of Health, American women have a 1:40 chance of having twins and a 1:539 chance of giving birth to triplets.
- In 2001, 121,246 sets of twins were born in the United States.
- In that same year, there were 6,885 triplet births, and 501 cases of quadruplet births.
- Only eighty-five of all births in 2001 were births of five or more babies.

Did You Know...?

- Twins are more frequently born in the western world than in the eastern.

- "Siamese Twins" (née conjoined twins) were given the label because of the celebrated Chang and Eng Bunker born at Meklong, on May 11, 1811 of Chinese parents.
- The first set of U.S.-born septuplets occurred on May 21, 1985. They were born to Patti Jorgensen Frustaci of Orange, California, who was taking fertility drugs.
- There are three women across the globe who have given birth to septuplets, all of whom survived.

Tiny Tots

The lightest recorded combined weight of surviving twins was 2 lb., 3 oz., in the case of Mary and Margaret Stimson of Peterborough, England.

The Long and the Short of It

- Mrs. Danny Berg of Rome, Italy, gave birth to a baby girl, Diana, on December 23, 1987—but twin sister Monica did not arrive until January 30, 1988, and then only by Caesarean section.
- The fastest recorded natural birth of triplets took two minutes, when Mrs. James E. Duck of Memphis, Tennessee gave birth to Bradley, Christopher, and Carmon on March 21, 1977.

Quotable Mom

"The mother loves her child most divinely, not when she surrounds him with comfort and anticipates his wants, but when she resolutely holds him to the highest standards and is content with nothing less than his best."
—Hamilton Wright Mabie (American writer, 1845-1916)

Multiply This

A fifty-two-year-old Italian grandmother recovered in a Naples hospital after giving birth naturally to triplets. Antonietta Mellone, who already had three grown children, said she had never used fertility treatment. The boy and two girls, Gabriele, Alessia, and Nunzia, were born seven weeks premature. They weighed in at between 2.4 lbs. and 3.7 lbs.

Quotable Mom

"God could not be everywhere, and therefore He made mothers."
—Jewish Proverb

If At First You Don't Succeed...

One mother said she had her heart set on having twins—even though she already had nine children and another on the way. Helen Ogiliev, 41, of Denton, Manchester, who was five months pregnant, said she was determined to keep trying until she had twins.

Mrs. Ogiliev, whose children were aged between one and twenty-one years old, told the *Daily Mail* that she's always been fascinated by twins. "I can't believe that after so many pregnancies I haven't had twins. I was disappointed when I had my latest scan and found I was only carrying one baby," she said. Husband Stuart, forty-four, a caterer, said he'd come to terms with her ambition: "Every time we have another one, she promises me it will be our last," he said.

The Waltons Had Nothing On These Families

An eighteenth century peasant woman from Shuya, one-hundred-and-fifty miles east of Moscow, holds the record for the most children.

- Between 1725 and 1765, in twenty-seven confinements, she gave birth to sixty-nine children.

- Her brood included sixteen pairs of twins, seven sets of triplets, and four sets of quadruplets; sixty-seven survived infancy.

- Currently, Leontina, Albina is the most prolific mother, having produced fifty-five children, including five sets of triplets.

- The oyster still wins, though. Over her lifetime, a female oyster may produce over a hundred million young.

Can You Say... Fast?

An American woman gave birth to sextuplets—all born within sixty seconds. Jennifer Hanselman delivered Ohio state's first set of sextuplets at Akron General Medical Center. Doctors say the three boys and three girls, ranging in weight from 1 lb., 9 oz. to 2 lbs., 10 oz., were in relatively good health.

They showed no signs of major complications or disabilities, reported the Akron Beacon Journal. Dr. Justin Lavin said: "When we started taking the babies out, they just kept coming one after another. It was a pretty exciting experience." Their father, Keith Hanselman, said the rapid-fire births were "pretty overwhelming. It was like a popcorn popper."

Like Mother Like Daughter

A mother and daughter gave birth to sons on the same day and in the same hospital. Eighteen-year-old Amy Cossey was first into the delivery room of the Norfolk and Norwich University Hospital. She had gone into labor in the early hours of the morning and gave birth three hours later to baby Harvey. Her mother Kim Roberts was asleep down the corridor after being admitted the previous day. Fourteen hours later Kim, forty-two, gave birth herself to Haydn at the hospital in Norwich, reported the *Daily Mail*.

Triple Play

In October 2003, Fatma Saygi, twenty-eight, from the Turkish province of Adiyaman and Fatma, gave birth to her sixth set of triplets. Saygi, who gave birth to her first three children at the age of eighteen, said: "We wanted children but we didn't really want that many. But Allah has always given us three at a time." The family of seventeen lives in a two-room flat and on an income of about £12 a week, which her husband, Mehmet, earns as a wedding singer.

Turning Tragedy to Life

When Peggy Spies of Austin, Texas, delivered a stillborn baby after only twenty-one weeks of pregnancy, she knew her milk would soon come in and that it would be valuable to others. "I learned 'preemie' milk is even more rare and valuable than full-term mother's milk and decided to donate," Spies said.

Not only would she be helping others, Spies reasoned, but putting the milk to good use would help her grieve for her dead child. So the busy mother of three paused six times each day at her job with the Texas General Land Office. She went to a private area and used a breast pump for twenty minutes. Over the next six weeks, she produced 673 ounces of breast milk, which she donated to the Mother's Milk Bank in Austin, Texas.

3

Motherhood through the Ages

Lucy, The Mother of Man (and Woman)

In 1974, anthropologist Donald Johanson found a female skeleton in northern Ethiopia. The archeologists dubbed the remains "Lucy" after the Beatles' song "Lucy in the Sky With Diamonds," the tune that was playing in the camp as the successful excavation team celebrated its discovery.

Lucy is estimated to be 3.2 million years old. Johanson named her species Australopithecus afarensis, which means "southern ape of Afar," after the Ethiopian region where Lucy was found.

Like a chimpanzee, Lucy had a small brain, long dangly arms, short legs, and a large belly. But she was no ape. Like humans, Lucy was bipedal—she routinely walked upright on two legs. This characteristic puts Lucy in the human family.

Did You Know...?

While the average weight of a newborn today is about seven pounds, the average weight of a Homo rudolfensis baby (a human ancestor of about two million years ago) is estimated to have been 4.6 pounds.

Quotable Mom

"If evolution really works, how come mothers only have two hands?" —Milton Berle, actor

Motherhood in the Ancient World

Under-population in the Greek and Roman empires was a major problem. As a result, women were highly valued for their ability to give birth to generations of much-needed laborers and soldiers. In this pre-Christian era, pagan priesthood celebrated fertility, and bearing children received the highest glory.

❀
Did You Know...?

Contrary to popular belief, Julius Caesar was probably not born by Caesarean Section. Caesar's mother, Aurelia, lived long after the birth of her son, and it is highly unlikely that she would have survived such a surgery. What is more, in Roman times surgical removal of babies was used only in the event that the mother was dead or dying. Indeed, Roman law under Caesar decreed that all women who faced death in childbirth must have surgery to remove their unborn child.

It is this law, intended to bolster the Roman population, that is probably why the procedure is called "caesarian." Until the sixteenth and seventeenth centuries the procedure was known as caesarean operation; the term "section" was first used in 1598 by Jacques Guillimeau is his book on midwifery. ❀

Blended Family in Rome

Mark Antony had a number of colorful wives, including his unofficial dalliance with Cleopatra, the Queen of Egypt. One of the most famous mothers of the Roman era was Octavia, the surviving wife of Mark Antony.

Antony was officially married to Fulvia who lived in Rome with their two sons. That didn't stop Mark Antony from becoming involved with Cleopatra. The two spent the winter of 40-41 BC together in Alexandria and their relationship produced twins, Alexander and Cleopatra. When his Roman wife, Fulvia, died,

Antony was compelled to shore up his political affairs in Rome by marrying again. He returned to Rome for his wedding to Octavia, the sister of Octavius, a staunch political rival.

For several years, Antony maintained his two marriages—his unofficial one to Cleopatra, and his official union with Octavia, which resulted in two daughters. Increasingly, however, Antony favored his marriage with Cleopatra, and in 35 BC he divorced Octavia. The divorce greatly angered Octavius and he declared war against his former brother-in-law.

Antony and Cleopatra fled to Alexandria. Facing certain death at the hands of Octavius' soldiers, the couple did what any good Roman would do—they committed suicide. After their deaths, Octavia established one of the first blended households. Remarkably, she raised all of Antony's children—their two daughters, the twins of he and Cleopatra, the two sons he had with Fulvia, and her own children from her previous marriages—all under the same Roman roof.

Quotable Mom

"All women become like their mothers. That is their tragedy. No man does. That is his." —Oscar Wilde

Medieval Mom Gives Birth

In the middle ages, motherhood was the most important social role for women, and it was seen as the fulfillment of God's will for women. So important was motherhood that numerous couples did not even marry until the woman had proven her fertility. Contraception was very much frowned upon by the church, and women commonly had seven or eight children.

There was no anesthetic, and child and mother mortality rates were high. Women gave birth in a lying-in room, where they would usually be accompanied by women only. Wealthy women would be aided by midwives, and poor women by their female relatives. Male physicians would attend the birth only where surgery was deemed necessary.

Unlucky

Because it was considered unlucky, new fathers did not attend births. To ease the pain and speed delivery, midwives would rub the mother's belly with ointment. Birth was expected in twenty contractions. If it took longer, superstition would be employed to speed up the process. Throughout the household, doors and windows would be opened—an act that symbolized the opening of the womb.

After the birth, medieval women convalesced in lying-in rooms. Lying-in rooms could get crowded with midwives, female relatives, and visitors stopping by to give their regards to the new mom. For six weeks after giving birth, women were prohibited from attending church.

Medieval Baptism

In the superstitious middle ages, baptism was extremely important, and babies were baptized on the day they were born. The purpose of baptism was to wash away original sin and free the child from evil. It was so important that the early Catholic Church empowered midwives to conduct the sacrament out of fear that a newborn might die without the rite.

Medieval baptism also served an important social function. The rite conferred upon the new baby its name. It also established a life-long link between the baby and its godparents, who would be responsible for the child's spiritual well-being.

*"How simple a thing it seems to me that to know ourselves
as we are, we must know our mothers names."*
—Alice Walker, writer

A REMARKABLE MEDIAEVAL MOM:
CHRISTINE DE PISAN, 1364-1430

Though she was born in Venice in 1364, Christine de Pisan
spent her formative years in France living with her father,
Thomas de Pisan, an astrologer to Charles V. Christine had a
privileged, educated upbringing that came with life in the royal
court. At fifteen, she married Estienne deCastel. In 1390, the
Great Plague claimed Estienne's life and left Christine widowed
at just twenty-four years of age.

She was left to support herself, her three young children, and
her aging mother. To do so, Christine turned to a profession not
typically available to fourteenth century women: she took up
writing and wrote prose and poetry, which in particular proclaimed the need for women's equality.

Wildly popular, Christine de Pisan is commonly recognized as
the first woman in western literature to make a living by her
pen. Though driven into a literary world typically not the domain
of women, motherhood was also a role she held dear. In a poem
for her son, Christine offered advice to her children:

*I have no great fortune, my son,
To make you rich. In place of one
Here are some lessons I have learned—
the finest things I've ever earned.*

Before the world has borne you far,
Try to know people as they are.
Knowing that will help you take
The path that keeps you from mistake.

Pity anyone who is poor
And stands in rags outside your door
Help them when you hear them cry!
Remember that you, too, will die.

Love those who have love for you
And keep your enemy in view:
Of allies none can have too many,
Small enemies there are not any.

Never lose what the good Lord gave
To this, our world too much enslaved:
The foolish rush to end their lives.
Only the steadfast soul survives.

Quotable Mom

*"One of the oldest human needs is having someone to
wonder where you are when you don't come home at night."*
—Margaret Mead, anthropologist

Motherhood in Early America

The first mothers of European descent arrived in North
America in 1620. Seeking religious freedoms, the "pilgrims,"
as they came to be known, made a perilous two-month journey
across the Atlantic.

Mayflower Moms

On September 6, 1620, the Mayflower left Plymouth, England. On November 11, 1620, the ship carrying 102 passengers and thirty crew landed on the east coast of North America. Three of those who left England were pregnant moms-to-be who were in their third trimester.

- While still at sea, Elizabeth Hopkins gave birth to a son, appropriately named Oceanus.

- Shortly after landfall, Susanna White also gave birth to a son, Peregrine, whose name appropriately means "one who journeys to foreign lands."

- The third pregnant mom, Mary Allerton, sadly gave birth to a stillborn son as houses were being built at Plymouth Colony.

Mothers of the Revolution

In early America, motherhood was the central role of women. A woman was considered the "softer sex," deemed to be inferior to men, and created to serve her husband and nurture her children. Blocked from public life, married women were expected to shine in the home. In addition to caring for her kids, moms were responsible for growing and preparing food, making cloth and clothing, and maintaining the household.

From 1775-1783 Americans fought to free themselves from two centuries of British rule. As revolutionary ideals spread, mothers were expected not only to share their husband's political ideals, but to impart them to their children. In addition, some moms became more directly involved in the war, even serving in battle, despite a prohibition against women's military involvement.

Revolutionary Moms

- Deborah Samson disguised herself as a man so that she could serve in Washington's Army in the American Revolution. To conceal her identity, Sampson tended to her own battle wounds. After the war, Samson married Benjamin Gannett and mothered three children.

- Mary Lindley Murray and her charming daughters, especially young Beulah and Susannah, kept British forces entertained and distracted, allowing 4,000 patriot soldiers to escape to safety.

- Sybil Ludington, the so-called "female Paul Revere," was just a teenager when she rode throughout the night calling minutemen to arms and saving her town. She later had one son.

- Patience Wright, an American sculptor working in London, spied on the British and sent secret dispatches to the colonies in her artwork. At the time of her covert activities, she was a widow raising five children on her own.

- Molly Pitcher tended a cannon after her husband was wounded in battle. Her heroic deeds inspired patriot troops to fight on. Molly had at least one son, also a war hero, who distinguished himself in the war of 1812.

Quotable Mom

"Every mother is like Moses. She does not enter the promised land. She prepares a world she will not see." —Pope Paul VI

Moms and Slavery

Female slaves were not expected to be "mothers," but rather expected to "breed"—to produce more slaves for their masters. In each year between 1750 and the Civil War, more than 20 percent of women slaves of childbearing ages bore children.

Slave owners manipulated black women into having children using a system of rewards that reduced workloads for pregnant women and increased their food allotments. For women who resisted these "positive" incentives, the threat of whippings and sale were used to coerce slave women to give birth.

After the birth, female slaves were expected to return to the fields, sometimes carrying their infants on their backs. If they attended too frequently to their children, they risked punishment by whipping. Not surprisingly, motherhood increased women's resolve to escape their enslavement. It is no coincidence that in 1850, one-hundred-fifty fugitive women had fled to New Orleans with their children.

Sadly, fleeing with children increased the odds of being captured. According to William Still, the head of the Philadelphia Underground Railroad, "Females undertook three times the risk of failure [to escape] that males were liable to." But one can imagine why these brave women would be driven to flee. The anguish of a mother who had to witness the brutalization of her children or their "sale" by auction to the highest bidder is utterly unimaginable today.

❀

Frontier Mom

When the American west was opened to settlement in the mid-nineteenth century, wives and mothers accompanied their husbands to isolated climes where they together sought to eke out their livelihoods. On the frontier, families didn't have the "luxury" of distinct roles—women, like men, worked in the fields and hunted. Children were welcomed into frontier families—for children provided a valuable army of labor on fledgling farms.

Missouri families in the mid-nineteenth century had, on average, a child once every two years, and ten children in all. On the frontier, childbirth was especially dangerous. Physicians and midwives were scarce, and laboring mothers often had no assistance except that of their husbands or older daughters.

Mothers who survived birth found frontier lives with small children to be psychologically trying. Often, moms missed the family and support networks they had left behind, and they acutely felt the lack of female companionship that frontier life granted.

MARY RICHARDSON WALKER

One of the first non-Native moms to live in the western United States was Mary Richardson Walker. Walker had studied theology at the Maine Wesleyan Seminary and, with graduation under her belt and a new husband to boot, she had one big dream to fulfill—to spread the word of God in the wild west.

In 1830, the newlyweds struck out on the 3000-mile trek to Oregon. Mary quickly got pregnant, and her account of the birth of her firstborn reflects her fatigue, fear, and hope.

She wrote of the birth: "Just as I supposed the worst was yet to come, my ears were saluted by the cry of my child and I soon forgot my misery." As Mary and her husband spread the word of God, she bore six more children.

KITTURAH (KIT) PENTON BELKNAP

One of the first moms to make a home on the western frontier was Kit Belknap, who traveled with her husband from Iowa to take up a homestead in Oregon. Before Kit and her husband George left on their western journey in 1847, Kit had borne four children. Only the youngest, a one-year-old son named Jesse, had survived. Kit wrote in her diary, "Now we have one little baby left, so I will spend what little strength I have left getting ready to cross the Rockies."

The trip was grueling. Kit herself was pregnant again and sickness dogged them at every turn. At one point, Kit feared her sole surviving son, stricken with "Mountain Fever," would die on the trail. They all survived, however, and Kit, her son, and husband made it to Oregon, where her new baby was born, and they went on to raise five children.

Klondike Mom

On August 16, 1896, gold was found in Rabbit Creek, near Dawson, in the Yukon territory. Promptly renamed Bonanza Creek, locals began staking claims in the hopes of striking it rich. Gold was everywhere, and the world knew it. More than one hundred thousand gold-seekers struck out for the Klondike on dangerous westbound trails.

Among these were approximately one thousand women. Mothers held a revered place in gold rush settlements. In communities dominated by the single men who worked the mines, families with children were a rarity. So rare were children, that in the Fourth of July parade held at Nome, Alaska, in 1900, one of the main attractions was a decorated baby carriage holding the first white baby born in the community.

Marrying for Love

Somewhere between the American Revolution and the first decades of the 1800s, the institution of marriage was revolutionized. Love, and not considerations of property and social status, became the key consideration in choosing a spouse.

The Rights of Victorian Women Concerning Their Children

Victorian moms continued to be housekeepers, of course, but increasingly they were expected to take on a much more pronounced moral leadership role. Mothers were responsible for not just the physical, but also the moral and spiritual well-being of their children and husbands. Until her husband's premature death left her a grieving widow for fifty years, Queen Victoria represented this motherly ideal.

Despite a woman's role as spiritual guide for her children, legally they had no rights to their children. Under the law, men were considered the sole custodians. In the rare case of divorce, even one caused by a husband's abuse or adultery, a mother could be denied all rights to see her children.

Take Five: The Top Five Most Popular Boy Baby Names in the 1890s

1. John
2. William
3. James
4. George
5. Charles

The Top Five Most Popular Baby Girl Names in the 1890s

1. Mary
2. Anna
3. Elizabeth
4. Emma
5. Margaret

Source: Compiled from U.S. Social Security registration information for the 1890s.

Suffragist Mom

In the United States, the suffragist movement began in the mid-nineteenth century with women challenging the commonly held notion that they lacked the intellectual capacity for full political participation.

The suffragist movement employed a number of arguments, and one of the most powerful used the concept of motherhood. As mothers, they argued, they were compelled to act publicly to put an end to the ills and evils of society. Motherhood, they argued, was an important occupation that could protect society against injustice and discord. In a sense, they were arguing that society needed to be "mothered" by its women. In order to effectively do so, however, women must have the vote.

The Victories

 In 1869, two American feminist leaders created the independent National Woman Suffrage Association, the main objective of which was to secure women's right to vote. This group worked on a state-by-state basis, and in 1869 Wyoming became the first state to enact women's suffrage. Their efforts redoubled in 1890 when suffragists formed the National American Woman Suffrage Association, a body to agitate for suffrage at the state and federal levels.

Thanks to their work, several states joined Wyoming in providing for women's suffrage and in 1910 the association gathered 500,000 signatures on a petition urging federal woman-suffrage legislation.

The American suffragist movement scored its major victory just after World War I. In 1919, the U.S. Congress approved the 19th Amendment to the U.S. Constitution. It provided that "The right of citizens of the United States to vote shall not be denied or abridged by the United States or by any State on account of sex."

ELIZABETH CADY STANTON, 1815-1902

Elizabeth Stanton is one of the best-known suffragists and women's right activists of the nineteenth century. What is less known is that she was also the mother of seven children. Born the daughter of a wealthy New York lawyer in 1815, she was one of five surviving children who grew up hearing of the legal hardships faced by the women her father represented. At sixteen, Elizabeth left school, and at twenty-four she met and fell in love with fellow abolitionist Henry B. Stanton.

After a turbulent engagement in which Elizabeth questioned the prospect of marriage, in May of 1840 the two were married in a ceremony that purposely excluded the traditional vow of obedience. When Stanton gave birth to her first child soon after marriage, she proved to be an extremely progressive mother for her times. She refused to swaddle her infant, as was the dangerous custom of the day. And she nursed her own baby, feeding the child every two hours and trusting her "mother's instinct."

❦

HELLO SENECA

When she and Henry moved their growing brood from Boston to Seneca Falls, she was overwhelmed with her motherly duties, particularly given the frequent absences of her husband. In a lament familiar to moms today, she remarked:

"To keep a house and grounds in good order, purchase every article for daily use, keep the wardrobes of a half dozen human beings in proper trim, take the children to dentists, shoemakers, and different schools, and to find teachers at home, altogether made such sufficient work to keep one's brain busy, as well as all the hands I could press into service. Then too, the novelty of housekeeping had passed away, and much that was once attractive in domestic life was now irksome."

Her discontent fueled her activism, and from 1850 onward she teamed up with her close friend, Susan B. Anthony, to raise to the American public issues affecting women in general, and the issue of their suffrage in particular. With writings, speeches, as a candidate for Congress, and as a long-serving president of the National Woman Suffrage Association, Stanton was one of the most important advocates of women's rights. Although Stanton died in 1902, years before women would get the vote, her activism was the bedrock of women's road to political equality.

Quotable Mom

"Poor baby…a woman's lot is so hard!" —Anne Roelofson
These words inspired her daughter, Abigail Jane Scott,
a suffragist, activist, and mother.

Did You Know…?

The first American woman to vote under the 19th Amendment (the suffrage amendment which legally gave American women the right to vote) was Mrs. Marie Ruoff Byrum. She cast her ballot in a by-election for city alderman in Hannibal, Missouri, at 7 a.m. on August 31, 1920.

Motherhood in the 1930s

In October, 1929, the bottom fell out of the North American stock market, taking the fortunes of many Americans with it as it crashed. At the nadir of the depression in 1933, one-third of Americans were, according to President Roosevelt, "ill-housed, ill-clad, and ill-nourished." The worst economic crisis that the country ever experienced demanded mothers' resourcefulness and creativity to ensure that they and their loved ones survived.

The Original Spam

When the recession hit, mothers faced new challenges. Responsible for feeding their families even amidst dire poverty, moms devised new and ingenious recipes to stretch scarce food resources. Popular dishes of the 1930s included inexpensive, one-dish meals such as casseroles. Fueled by this concern for economy, Hormel developed Spam, a cheap, versatile canned meat product that became an American staple and standard fare for American moms seeking to feed their families on a budget.

Great Stork Derby

In October, 1926, a quirky Canadian lawyer well known for his off-the-wall sense of humor, died suddenly of a heart attack. As eccentric in death as he had been in life, the last will and testament of Charles Vance Millar generated a decade of excitement for moms living in Canada's largest city of Toronto.

In a bizarre clause of his last will and testament, Millar left a huge portion of his considerable fortune to the Toronto woman who had the most babies in the decade following his death. Of course, Millar could not have known that the world was about to plunge into recession when he started his baby race, known as the "stork derby." But when times got hard, Toronto women took the contest seriously...after all, the $750,000 dollars up for grabs was no small sum, especially in the "dirty thirties."

And The Winner Is

The ten-year contest was marked by political in-fighting and court challenges. One contestant, Pauline Clarke, gave the contest her best shot, bearing ten children in ten years. The fact that her children had different fathers did not go over well in the morally conservative city and she was disqualified. Another "contestant," Lillian Kenney, was disqualified when several of her twelve children who died in childbirth were not counted in her total. The prize ended up being split between four contestants who had each given birth to ten children in the decade. Kenney and Clarke were given $12,500 for what the committee called their "effort."

The Dionne Quintuplets

Perhaps the most famous mom of the "dirty thirties" was Elzire Dionne, who gave birth to the world's first surviving identical quintuplets on May 28, 1934, during the depths of the difficult 1930s. The wife of a poor farmer, Oliva, Elzire was already the mother of six children aged two to seven when she gave birth to what became her most famous children.

The family was broadsided by the shock of the multiple births and the burden of feeding five more mouths. Their modest home, which lacked running water and electricity, was hardly the place for five small babies who needed special care.

In September, as soon as they could safely be moved, the government took custody of the children and relocated them to a specially built nursery, ostensibly to ensure the children's health. The quints, however, rapidly became a tourist attraction and a cash cow for the province, raking in millions for provincial coffers.

The nursery evolved into "Quintland," which included a school with a playground, observation decks, and souvenir shops. For nine years the five girls lived at Quintland, subjected to the prying eyes of three million tourists—including the King and Queen of England—who were seeking a glimpse of the young medical marvels. After a protracted custody battle, Elzire and Oliva won custody of their children and the girls returned home.

The Mother Road

In *The Grapes of Wrath*, John Steinbeck christened the famous Route 66 as the "Mother Road," the path of hope followed by those families whose mettle was tested by the Great Depression. During the 1930s, desperate families who were displaced from the drought and starvation of the Dust Bowl packed up their cars and traveled the Mother Road to California in search of opportunity.

Modern Momma

After the economic recession of the 1930s, and World War II, American women were eager to reestablish "normalcy" in their lives and many eagerly turned to motherhood. Between 1947 and 1957, America experienced an astounding "baby boom." The number of babies born each year rose from 2.5 million to 4.1 million.

Instruction for Moms

As America sought to make its way in the post-war era, a woman's role as "mother" was much vaunted. Women were encouraged to leave the factories they had occupied during the war and to return to their homes and free up jobs for returning servicemen.

As soldiers returned from the front, the "bread winner" ideal grew popular. Accordingly, men were expected to be the bread winners, and women to become full-time mothers. Her "work" was that of the home, and she was charged with the task of raising her family. Enter the picket fence and the suburban home, both idealized as the peaceful haven of full-time moms and their families.

Dr. Benjamin Spock was one of the foremost experts on the new modern mom that emerged after World War II. Born in 1903 to a prominent lawyer and devoted mom, Spock's position as the oldest of seven children exposed him at an early age to the world of child care, as he helped his mom care for his younger siblings. Spock attended Yale, went on to graduate from Columbia University with a degree in medicine, and ended up specializing in pediatrics. Keen to attend to the psychological needs of his young patients, Spock turned his study to psychoanalysis and came to realize that the prevailing wisdom about child care was fundamentally flawed. In 1946, Spock published his now famous *The Common Sense Book of Baby and Child*, selling the book to women eager to embrace their role as mothers for a mere 25 cents a copy.

In an era in which child care was being medicalized and control being wrested away from parents and placed in the hands of child care "professionals," Spock reminded parents that they were the authority on the well-being of their children. He stressed that parenthood could and should be an enjoyable experience, and he gave them the commonsense advice to carry out that task.

In the 1960s, 1970s, and 1980s, Spock's vocal stance against the Vietnam War, and later against nuclear armament, harmed book sales, but he felt these issues to be of paramount importance for parents and children. Spock had two children of his own, sons Michael and John, with his first wife, Jane Cheney.

Some Tips on Motherhood
(or caring for your biggest baby)

Excerpts from *How to be a Good Wife*, home economics high school text book, 1954:

- Have dinner ready. Plan ahead, even the night before, to have a delicious meal, on time. This is a way of letting him know that you have been thinking about him and are concerned about his needs. Most men are hungry when they come home and the prospect of a good meal is part of the warm welcome needed.

- Prepare yourself. Take fifteen minutes to rest so that you'll be refreshed when he arrives. Touch up your makeup, put a ribbon in your hair and be freshlooking. He has just been with a lot of work-weary people. Be a little gay and a little more interesting. His boring day may need a lift.

- Clear away the clutter. Make one last trip through the main part of the home just before your husband arrives, gather up schoolbooks, toys, paper, etc. Then run a dust cloth over the tables. Your husband will feel he has reached a haven of rest and order, and it will give you a lift, too.

- Prepare the children. Take a few minutes to wash the children's hands and faces (if they are small), comb their hair, and if necessary, change their clothes. They are little treasures and he would like to see them playing the part.

- Minimize all noise. At the time of his arrival, eliminate all noise of the washer, dryer, dishwasher, or vacuum. Try to encourage the children to be quiet. Be happy to see him. Greet him with a warm smile and be glad he is home.

- Some don'ts: Don't greet him with problems or complaints. Don't complain if he is late for dinner. Count this as minor compared with what he might have gone through that day.

Make him comfortable. Have him lean back in a comfortable chair or suggest he lie down in the bedroom. Have a cool or warm drink ready for him. Arrange his pillow and offer to take off his shoes. Speak in a low, soft, soothing, and pleasant voice. Allow him to relax and unwind.

- Listen to him. You may have a dozen things to tell him, but the moment of his arrival is not the time. Let him talk first.

- Make the evening his. Never complain if he does not take you out to dinner or to other places of entertainment. Instead, try to understand his world of strain and pressure, his need to be home and relax.

- The Goal: Try to make your home a place of peace and order where your husband can renew himself in body and spirit.

Quotable Mom

"...Her career is the most important one a woman can choose...Her job is to keep her family well fed and patched and clean behind the ears. Her ambition is to build good citizens...to make them happy and comfortable and proud of the way they live. Her working day often begins before dawn and may last right up until bedtime—seven days a week. Her pay? The pay she values most is the loving appreciation of her family."
—General Mills cookie advertisement

The "Second Oldest Profession": Moms Raising Kids

"I really learned it all from mothers."
—Dr. Benjamin Spock, child-rearing expert

"'Mother' has always been a generic term synonymous with love, devotion and sacrifice…Motherhood is the second oldest profession in the world. It never questions age, height, religious preference, health, political affiliation, citizenship, morality, ethnic background, marital status, economic level, convenience or previous experience. It's the biggest on-the-job training program in existence today."
—Erma Bombeck, *Motherhood: The Second Oldest Profession*

State of the Union

Not only is motherhood the second oldest profession for women in the world, it is also the most ubiquitous.

- According to the Bureau of the Census, 81 percent of U.S. women will become mothers in their lifetime.

- In the United States alone, there are 75 million moms with 83 million children.

- In all, 57 percent of American women are moms.

- The state with the greatest number of moms per capita is Kentucky, where a whopping 67 percent of women are moms.

- On average, American moms can expect to have two children in their lifetimes. Only 11 percent of moms end their child-bearing years with four or more children.

- Moms in Utah have the most babies; on average, Utah moms have three children.

Quotable Mom

"A mother is a person who, seeing there are only four pieces of pie for five people, promptly announces she never did care for pie."
—Tenneva Jordan

A Pricey Venture

Raising a family is not cheap, and it is getting more expensive by the year.

- According to the U.S. Department of Agriculture Center for Policy and Development, the average cost of raising an American child born in 1960 to age eighteen was (in 2000 dollars) $145,000.

- Meanwhile, the cost of raising a child born in 1999 to age eighteen was $165,630.

- Today, the cost of raising a child is $173,880 by the time they turn eighteen.

- Children are most expensive in their teen years, between ages fifteen and seventeen. Indeed, it is estimated that teenagers cost their parents $14,670 annually.

You Ate How Much?

The cost of cereal alone can break the parental bank when you consider that the average child will eat fifteen pounds of cereal in a year, according to allaboutmoms.com.

Quotable Mom

"Mother is the name of God in the lips and hearts of children."
—*William Makepeace Thackeray*

If Mom Got Her Dues

- The United Nations Human Development Report estimated that women spend two-thirds of their time on unpaid work, and most of those hours are spent on caring work.

- If women's unpaid work was counted, it would contribute 11 trillion dollars to the world economy.

- Women's unremunerated work in the United States is valued at 1,491 billion dollars a year.

- Assuming that $8.00/hr is the current market rate for home-based child care, if a mom were to be paid for the fifty hours she spends caring for children each week, she would earn an annual income of $20,800, according to *Mothering Magazine*.

- If mom were paid for being a chauffeur, she would earn $3,120 a year—the same amount that she would be owed for doing a thorough house-cleaning each week.

Mr. Mom Myth

The media makes much of "Mr. Mom," but he remains an elusive figure in America. Of the 20.5 million children under age five in America, only 320,000 (1.5 percent) have a father as their primary guardian, according to *The Price of Motherhood: Why the Most Important Job in the World is Still the Least Valued.*

Take Five: Five Reasons Why Moms Get Up Early

1. Sports practices
2. Cartoons
3. Wet beds (not their own!)
4. Early morning kitchen disasters
5. Three's a crowd in bed

Quotable Mom

"A good mother is worth hundreds of schoolmasters."
—*George Herbert*

What Moms Do Best: Everything

Comedienne Roseanne Barr once observed: "I know how to do anything—I'm a Mom." No truer words have ever been spoken. Moms really can and usually do do anything and everything.

- Eighty percent of American children say that their moms usually do the cooking, according to a survey by the Whirlpool Foundation.

- Only 7 percent said that Dad does.

- Seventy-four percent said that mom usually does the laundry, while 5 percent said dad generally does this task.

- Sixty-two percent said that mom usually washes dishes—just 6 percent said dad usually does.

Quotable Mom

"My mother gave me a bumblebee pin when I started work. She said: 'Aerodynamically, bees shouldn't be able to fly. But they do. Remember that.'" —Jill E. Barad, CEO of Mattel

Wired Moms

- Sixty percent of children aged 7–12 say that mom is the best at using the computer, according to AOL Digital Marketing Services, Inc.

- Today, 16.4 million American moms are online.

- Perhaps because they see being connected as beneficial to the family, 53 percent of moms think that the World Wide Web has brought their family together, and 92 percent see the Internet as a good educational tool for their children.

- The Internet has significantly helped today's busy mothers save time. In fact, AOL finds that 80 percent of moms in the U.S. go online to do chores and other activities.

- Thirty percent of moms say they wish their mate knew how hard they work all day, according to a survey by *Sesame Street Parents* magazine.

Then And Now

- In 1936, American families preferred to have an average of 3.6 children, according to the Gallup Organization.

- Today, American families favor 2.5 children.

- The more things change, the more they stay the same. In 1965, mothers reported spending 5.3 hours a day with their children. Today, moms are spending 5.5 hours a day with their kids, according to Bianchi.

- In 1951, 48 percent of Americans said that their mom had the greatest impact on them growing up. Today, 53 percent give mom this due.

Kids Think Mom Is Doing A Good Job

Kids in America appreciate what their moms do for them.

- Sixty-nine percent of American kids say that mom is loving, according to a Roper Starch survey for the Whirlpool Foundation.

- Of kids aged 6–11 surveyed by Hallmark, 23 percent say that their favorite thing that mom does with them is "she plays with me."

Just Like Mom

Teenagers especially have warm words for all mom does. If imitation is the sincerest form of flattery, then moms ought to be flattered.

- According to a Harris Interactive poll, 68 percent of teenaged girls admit that they want to be like their mothers.

- Sixty-three percent of teenage girls would go to mom with a personal problem, rather than to a friend.

- Teens also say that mom is their key financial advisor. While 29 percent would go to Dad with their money issues, 43 percent say that mom is their main source of financial advice.

Quotable Mom

*"If you have never been hated by your child,
you have never been a parent."* —Betty Davis

"Cleaning your house while your kids are still growing is like clearing the driveway before it stops snowing." —Phyllis Diller

Did You Know...?

Paul Simon's hit song "Mother and Child Reunion" was not inspired by a touching reunion of a mother and child, at least not in the way one might think. Rather, it was "hatched" over a chicken and egg dish enjoyed by the singer at a restaurant in New York's Chinatown.

Take Five: Five Foods That Were Not In Your House Before You Became A Mom

1. Gerber products
2. Dinosaur-shaped anything
3. Smiley-faced potato product
4. Kool-Aid
5. Fruit Snacks (usually spelled "Froot")

Mothering Styles

A few famous moms epitomize certain mothering styles. How do American moms think their own mothering stacks up?

• According to a survey by Baby Center Inc., 55 percent of American moms think that their style compares to that of "June Cleaver."

• Twenty-eight percent say that they, like Hillary Clinton, are "career moms."

• Sixteen percent say they are "unconventional" like Madonna.

Doing A Good Job and Knowing It

• Eighty-one percent of American moms think they have perfected the act of juggling family and work, according to a *Child* magazine poll.

• Ninety-seven percent of moms think they set a good example to their children.

• Eight-two percent say their kids are well-behaved.

• Ninety-two percent say their kids are happy.

- Some moms even think they are doing a better job than their own moms did with them. Seventy-two percent say they have a better relationship with their daughter than they did with their own mom when they were kids, according to a "Generation Clinique" study.

Like What We Do

- Although it is true that 70 percent of American moms say that motherhood is more challenging than they thought it would be, a whopping 92 percent say that it is more rewarding than they had anticipated, according to survey of 749 mothers responding to a *Child* magazine poll.

- Moreover, 72 percent of moms say that they value spending most of their non-working hours with their kids. A *Sesame Street Parents* magazine found that 77 percent of moms think that the best thing about being a mom is having fun with their kids.

A Mother's Influence

A mom's example can have a profound influence on her children.

- Children are twice as likely to exercise if their moms also exercise, compared to children with sedentary moms, according to a Boston University study.

Quotable Mom

"A suburban mother's role is to deliver children obstetrically once, and by car forever after."
—*Peter De Vries*

Take Five: Five Books Read by Moms to Their Kids

1. *Charlotte's Web*
2. *Where the Wild Things Are*
3. *The Cat in the Hat*
4. *Little Red Riding Hood*
5. *Hansel and Gretel*

Uncle Sam's Definition

child monitor (domestic ser.): Observes and monitors play activities or amuses children by reading to or playing games with them. Prepares and serves meals or formulas. Sterilizes bottles and other equipment used for feeding infants. Assists children to dress and bathe. Accompanies children on walks or other outings. Washes and irons clothing. Keeps children's quarters clean and tidy. Cleans other parts of home…may be designated baby sitter (domestic ser.) when employed on daily or hourly basis.
—U.S. government's definition of child care in a private home

Good Advice

"Be nice to your kids. They choose your nursing home."
—*Anonymous*

Body Image

- Ninety-four percent of moms say that they have had a different self image since the birth of their babies, according to a survey by *Sesame Street Parents* magazine.

- Not surprisingly, mom's changing body causes some concern. According to a babycenter.com survey, 69.4 percent of moms want their pre-baby body back.

- Another area of concern? Sex. Thirty-one percent of new moms want their pre-baby sex lives back, too.

Take Five: Five Things Women Did Before They Were Mothers

1. Slept late.
2. Made plans for two nights in a row.
3. Drank wine with meals.
4. Ate ethnic food.
5. Spent time with "the girls" (none of whom were under twelve).

Take Five: Five Things Women Do Now That They Are Mothers

1. Eat French fries as a vegetable.
2. Track the plot of cartoons.
3. Refers to themselves in the third person as "mommy."
4. Regularly answer a string of ten "but why?" questions.
5. Clean up bodily fluids without flinching.

ROSE FITZGERALD KENNEDY, 1890-1995, ON MOTHERHOOD

"...as interesting or challenging as any honorable profession in the world."

Born in Boston in 1890 to city mayor John Fitzgerald and his wife Mary Joseph Hannon, Rose Elizabeth Fitzgerald was the very epitome of Boston Irish gentry. At the age of seventeen, Rose met the man who she called the love of her life, Joseph "Joe" Patrick Kennedy. The two wed in October 1914, and from that point on Rose Fitzgerald Kennedy embarked on the happiest, most successful—and the most heartbreaking—undertaking of her life: motherhood.

By the time she was thirty, Rose had borne three children; by the time she was forty-one, the brood would reach nine: five daughters and four sons. Over the ensuing years, the names of those offspring—Joseph (1915), John ("Jack", 1917), Rosemary (1918), Kathleen (1920), Eunice (1921), Patricia (1924), Robert (1925), Jean (1928), and Edward (1932)—have been woven into the fabric of American life.

A PROFESSION

Rose was extraordinarily proud of being a mother. "I looked on child rearing not only as a work of love and duty," she said, "but as a profession that was fully as interesting and challenging as any honorable profession in the world and one that demanded the best that I could bring to it."

And she had every right to be proud. Her children were handsome and successful and contributed much to their country. Sons Robert and Edward were both U.S. Senators, while John took the family's tradition of public service to new heights, becoming the thirty-fifth President of the United States.

Though it brought her much pleasure, motherhood would also bring Rose incredible heartbreak. She buried four children. "I tell myself that God gave my children many gifts—spirit, beauty, intelligence, the capacity to make friends and to inspire respect," she said. "There was only one gift he held back—length of life."

Quotable Mom

"When you are a mother, you are never really alone in your thoughts. You are connected to your child and to all those who touch your lives. A mother always has to think twice, once for herself and once for her child." —Sophia Loren

"Mothers all want their sons to grow up to be President, but they don't want them to become politicians in the process." —John F. Kennedy

M.O.M.

All moms' heads swivel when they hear a child say "Mom!" Here are some other things called MOM:

- Manned Orbiting Mission (NASA)
- Man-on-the-move (military slang)
- Microsoft Office Manager (Microsoft)
- Middle of the Month
- Milk of Magnesia
- Minutes of Meeting

5

Moms at Work

"The good mother, the wise mother...is more important to the community than even the ablest man; her career is more worthy of honor and is more useful to the community than the career of any man, no matter how successful." —Theodore Roosevelt

Labor Pains

Mothers have always coped with the pains of labor, but labor laws have historically been even more of a pain for American mothers.

- In 1919, the ILO created the first global standard aimed at protecting working women before and after childbirth. In the U.S., however, before 1978, an employer could legally refuse to hire a woman on the basis of her motherhood or pregnancy.

- It was not until 1993 that the Family and Medical Leave Act was signed into law, for the first time granting maternity leave as a right to American women. Before the Act was passed, 8 percent of moms were forced to switch jobs as a result of pregnancy.

Moms on the Job

- According to the AFL-CIO, 71.9 percent of women with children younger than 18, 77.9 percent of women with kids aged 6–17, and 6.8 percent of moms with kids age six or younger are in the workforce.

Fairy Gift

"I think, at a child's birth, if a mother could ask a fairy godmother to endow it with the most useful gift, that gift would be curiosity."
—Eleanor Roosevelt

How Much Mom Works

Working moms put in longer hours than do their women colleagues without children.

- According to the AFL-CIO, 66 percent of working moms work 40 or more hours a week .
- Only 60 percent of women without kids work more than forty hours a week.
- Twenty percent of moms with young children work overtime.

Women in Business

Forty-nine percent of women with MBAs and high-paying jobs have children, according to a survey by Catalyst.

KATHIE LEE: A SURVIVOR

Kathie Lee Epstein entered this world on August 16, 1953, in Paris, France. Kathie Lee's father, Aaron Leon Epstein, was an American naval officer and weekend jazz saxophonist and her mother, Joan (nee Cuttell), a former Naval secretary turned radio singer.

Kathie Lee and her two siblings, David and Michelle, spent their early years in France and other European countries before coming back to the U.S. A young Kathie Lee attended Methodist Sunday school, becoming a born-again Christian at the tender age of twelve. At seventeen, Kathie Lee won her state Junior Miss pageant, traveling to Mobile, Alabama to represent Maryland in the nationwide competition.

It was here her life took another turn: meeting Anita Bryant, a prominent Christian singer and co-host of the pageant, confirmed what she was seeing in television ministries. Gifford felt what Bryant was doing was manipulation, and she was having none of it.

In 1976, as a brash twenty-three year old, Kathie Lee penned her personal thoughts about the ministries and eventually published those writings as *The Quiet Riot*. In the same year Gifford married her bible study group leader and the owner of a Christian music publishing company. Between 1976 and 1978, she recorded three gospel albums and the couple often appeared on religious television shows together. The marriage would crumble, however, under the pressure of a growing career.

DAY OF OUR LIVES
During these years, Kathie Lee also worked on her secular career, acting on *Days of Our Lives*, singing on commercial

jingles, and acting in several TV pilots. Gifford's time as the featured singer on *Name That Tune* led to a slew of opportunities, including the one that would make her a household name: co-host of *The Morning Show* in New York with Regis Philbin.

Kathie Lee took her seat next to Regis in June of 1985 and the two were an immediate success. On October 18, 1986, things got even better when she married ABC's Monday Night Football sports broadcaster and former NFL star, Frank Gifford. In 1988, *Live with Regis & Kathie Lee* became nationally syndicated. What soon arrived were what she called her two greatest achievements, Cody Newton, born in 1990, and Cassidy Erin, born in 1993.

In show business what goes up must come down, and down it came with a thud for Kathie Lee. She was plagued by a series of scandals in 1996 and 1997, first involving sweat-shop labor in factories making clothing with her endorsement, and later Frank's infidelity. Quickly responding to the controversies, Kathie Lee rose above them and since leaving her *Live* co-hosting duties (to spend more time with her family), she has recorded a number of pop-song and children's albums. She is simply a mother who has never quit.

Maternity Leave: A Global Perspective

Around the globe, governments are increasingly taking action to ensure that mothers are welcome in the workforce and that their maternity is valued and protected by laws allowing time off work at the birth of a baby. One-hundred-twenty nations now have legislation entitling new moms to paid maternity and health leave.

Then And Now

- Between 1961 and 1964, 10.1 percent of moms worked right up until the birth of their first child, and 9.9 percent were working again three months after their babies were born, according to the book Continuity and Change in the American Family.

- The latest available data shows that 35.1 percent of moms now work up until the birth of their first child and 40.9 percent were working at three months after giving birth.

Mom's At Work

- Seventy percent of men in their twenties grew up with a working mom.

- Only 32 percent of men age sixty-five or older, however, grew up in a home with a working mom, according to *Working Mother* magazine.

Quotable Mom

"The most remarkable thing about my mother is that for 30 years she served nothing but leftovers. The original meal has never been found." —Calvin Trillin

Bringing Home the Bacon

- Around the world, 30 percent of all households depend primarily on the salary of a woman, according to a UN report.

- According to *Working Mother* magazine, 55 percent of working moms earn the same as their spouses and 16 percent earn more than their spouses.

- All total, women manage household economies at an astounding rate. Eighty-five percent of all household income is managed by women.

Moms Who Work Have Kids Who Work

While 62 percent of kids who have stay-at-home moms clean their own rooms, 76 percent of the children of working moms complete this chore, according to a RoperStarch Worldwide survey.

Mutual Admiration Society

- Fifty-six percent of working mothers say they admire at-home moms.

- At-home moms return the compliment: almost 49 percent of stay-at-home moms say they admire moms who work, according to a survey by the Whirlpool Foundation.

Why Women Work

American moms work for a variety of reasons:

- According to Roper Starch Worldwide, 40 percent of moms think of work as a refuge away from home.

- Meanwhile, 53 percent of moms work "to pay those darn bills."

What Kids Think

American kids are realists when it comes to money.

- According to a survey by *Newsweek*, 23 percent of them want their parents to earn more of it.

But they are also aware of the impact of work on their moms.

- While 34 percent of kids want their mom to be less tired or stressed by work, fully 42 percent say that their moms enjoy what they do.

Mothers-At-Law

- In 1983, 81 percent of female lawyers said that it was "very" or "somewhat" realistic to combine the role of lawyer with that of wife and mother, according to a survey conducted by the ABA Journal. In 2000, 64.5 percent agreed.

Sacrifices

- Seventy-seven percent of working moms say they would stay home if they could, according to a survey by *Newsweek*.

- Mothers who do not work outside of the house devote, on average, 12.9 hours a week to undivided child care.

- Working moms, on the other hand, spend 6.6 hours a week on undivided child care, according to "Time for Life: The Surprising Ways Americans Use Their Time."

Sleep Deprived

- On average, working moms sleep five to six fewer hours a week than do moms who do not work.

- They also have twelve fewer hours of leisure time each week, according to the National Sleep Foundation.

- Seventy-four percent of moms who work outside the home say that " feeling tired all the time is a problem in their lives."

No Surprise

It's no surprise that motherhood can really put a dent in your disposable income. But it might also impede your earning potential.

- Mothers of a single child earn an average 2 percent less than working women who are not mothers.

- Moms of two children earn 13 percent less and moms of three children earn 22 percent less, according to a survey by the University of Pennsylvania's Population Studies Center.

Guilt

Working moms are often guilted into thinking they are neglecting their children. This, however, does not seem to be the case.

- In 1981, stay-at-home moms spent an average of twenty-six hours a week with their kids, according to the Institute for Social Research.

- Today, meanwhile, working moms managed to rack up an average of 26.5 hours spent with their children.

Single Mom

According to the Bureau of Census, 13.2 million families are headed by single mothers.

Child Care Costs

- On average, working moms with children aged 5–14 spend 6.6 percent of their incomes on child care, according to the Bureau of Census.

- Each week, employed moms spend an average of $81 to have their children cared for.

WORKING MOM: MARTHA STEWART

Born Martha Kostyra on August 3, 1941, in New Jersey, the woman who would later become famous as Martha Stewart was the second of six children of a working class family. Kostyra worked as a model from the age of thirteen, before attending Barnard College in Manhattan and earning a degree in European and Architectural History in 1962.

At Barnard, she also met a young Yale law student in the name of Andy Stewart. The two married in 1961 and soon had a daughter Alexis. Martha was not content to be at home though, going to work as a stockbroker on Wall Street.

In 1972, the family moved to Westport, Connecticut where they restored the nineteenth-century farmhouse they had bought. Energetic Martha couldn't, and wouldn't, stand still for long. She focused her energy on gourmet cooking, starting a catering business in the late 1970s, and soon the Stewart name became synonymous in New York with gourmet menus and unique, creative presentation.

MARTHA INC.

Stewart expanded into the world of publishing. Her first book, *Entertaining*, became a bestseller and was followed in quick succession by similar books. Within a decade, Martha Stewart, Inc., had grown into a million dollar business. Her newfound fame took its toll on her personal life, however, and her marriage to Andy Stewart ended in divorce in 1990.

In 1991, Martha Stewart, Inc., became Martha Stewart Living Omnimedia, Inc. Stewart's lifestyle empire soon grew to include two magazines, a checkout-size recipe publication, a popular cable television show, a syndicated newspaper column, a series of how-to books, a radio show, an Internet site, and $763 million in annual retail sales.

On October 19, 1999, America's most famous homemaker returned to Wall Street to see her company through its initial public offering on the New York Stock Exchange. In June 2002, Stewart again made financial headlines, this time for rumors of insider trading. Stewart was under investigation for selling hundreds of shares of ImClone Systems just prior to the Food and Drug Administration's refusal to approve the company's new cancer drug. In February 2004, a jury found her guilty of conspiracy, obstruction of justice, and two counts of making false statements.

Through it all, Stewart's daughter has been by her side. Stewart has served as a lightening rod for all manner of criticism, not the least of which is transforming the prevailing conception of the mother in the home. She has showcased not only the complete variety of skills needed in the home, but she has also demonstrated verve and creativity in carrying them out.

6

Moms Across Cultures

The experience of being a mom has been shared by women across all cultures and in all times. Around the world, however, cultural differences influence the way women approach and understand motherhood.

Moms in Malta

For Maltese moms, Catholic saints figure prominently in the birth experience. Expectant moms pray to Saint Raymond and Saint Spiridione for help in childbirth. During birth, many moms hold a statue of Saint Calogero. Saint Ludgarda is said to provide an easy delivery. Saint Blaise is said to protect new babies from throat diseases. In one Maltese village, moms-to-be used to drink water containing powder made from the bones of Saint Victor (the protective Saint of pregnant women) to ensure a smooth delivery. In another village, pregnant women wear the ring of Saint Peter the Martyr to avoid birth complications.

Take Five: Nations with the Top Five Birth Rates

1. Niger, 49.95
2. Mali, 48.37
3. Chad, 47.74
4. Uganda, 47.15
5. Somalia, 46.83

Take Five: Nations with the Five Lowest Birth Rates

1. Bulgaria, 8.05
2. Latvia, 8.27
3. Italy, 8.93
4. Estonia, 8.96
5. Germany, 8.99

Source: The World Fact Book (Births/1000 People)

Latvia

Latvians believe the goddess of Fate, known as Lamia, decides a baby's future from the moment of its birth. Latvian babies have traditionally been born in buildings called pirts, which are sauna-like steam baths. Three days after birth, babies and moms return to pirts for a ceremonial bathing, called a pirtizas. Nine days after the birth, they return again, and the baby receives a name and godparents in an elaborate, day-long ceremony called a Krustaba.

Everybody gathers around a grove of oak or birch trees, where guests are invited to share in a meal of bread, milk, cheese, and honey. The baby is submerged in water, as the clergy asks the godparents if they will accept the child and lift her into Mara's sun, or leave her in the water of the Mother of Spirits. The godmother then lifts the baby before a cross, while godparents all promise to care for the baby. At this point, the baby is assigned a name.

Orkney Islands Superstitions

One Orkney Island superstition has it that a bright rainbow predicts the birth of a baby boy, and that the newborn is to be found in the house at the end of the rainbow. Orkney islanders also believe that a mom should never reveal her pregnancy. Secrecy protects the baby from evil supernatural forces. Another belief is that a pregnant woman should sleep with a bible and knife under her bed to guard her unborn child. When the baby is born, these items will be placed in the baby's room to continue to offer protection.

Meal Madness

- In ancient Greece, if a mother's milk wasn't available, babies were fed a mixture of wine and honey from a terra-cotta banjo shaped vessel. Now that's gotta be better than mushed peas and carrots.

• In Victorian England, children were often fed "pap," a gruel-like mixture of water, cornmeal, and crushed walnuts. Sometimes flour, sugar, beer, wine, raw meat juices, and Castile soap were added to spruce it up a bit. We can't argue with that.

• Ancient Jews strictly enforced breast feeding and frowned on wet nurses or artificial means of feeding. Interestingly, there are several references to milk in the Old Testament, from Sarah nursing Isaac at age ninety, to the Promised Land described as "flowing with milk and honey."

Baby Names in Africa

Naming of babies in Africa is taken very seriously by new moms and dads. It is believed that names hold considerable power and will have a profound influence upon a child's life. The naming of a baby is a joyful event, one that welcomes the new child into his or her family and community.

In Nigeria, it is customary for the new parents to ask a grandfather or great-grandfather to choose the name. Traditionally, the name is chosen in a ceremony held on the seventh day after the baby's birth. At this ceremony, family and friends gather to pray for the child's well-being, health, and prosperity. After celebrating with prayer and food, the main naming ceremony takes place.

During the ceremony, the eldest female member of the family asks the baby's mother what she wants to call the baby. In response to the first six times she is asked, mom offers unthinkable names which are immediately rejected with song and music. When the question is asked the seventh time, the father of the child whispers the actual name to the mother who then announces it to the assembled crowd.

Take Five: Five Nigerian Names and Their Meanings

1. Onaiwu: This child will not die again.
2. Osamamianmianmwen: God did not forget me.
3. Ighiwiyisi: I shall not get lost in a foreign land.
4. Nowamagbe: He who is not harmed by members of his family cannot be harmed by outsiders.
5. Iyare: Safe journey.

Source: "Edo Naming Ceremony," Dr. Omoigu.

Alligator Power

- Alligator pepper is said to benefit the child's speech.

- Honey and sugar together with bitter kola nuts symbolize the child's life experiences.

- Salt symbolizes happiness.

- Water is important as it has no enemies.

- Palm oil will provide the grease to help the child through life's problems.

Rock-a-bye Baby...Singing Baby to Sleep Around the World

Mayo Mpapa: An African Lullaby

Mother carry me
I will care for you one day
It's not good to be alone in this world
Mother carry me
I will carry you one day
The way a crocodile carries its young on her back

Spi, Mladenets (Sleep My Baby):
A Traditional Russian Cossack Lullaby

Sleep my baby, my beautiful baby.
The beautiful moon is looking down on you.
Sleep little one, don't worry about anything
When the time comes you will know.

Fi la nana, e mi bel fiol:
Traditional Italian Lullaby

Hush-a-bye, my lovely child,
Hush-a-bye, my lovely child,
Hush, hush and go to sleep.
Hush, hush and go to sleep.

Sleep well, my lovely child,
Sleep well, my lovely child,
Hush, hush and go to sleep.
Hush, hush and go to sleep.

Duérmete Mi Niño:
Traditional Mexican Lullaby

Go to sleep my baby.
Go to sleep and dream,
for when you awaken
you shall have some cream.

Go to sleep my baby.
Go to sleep my sunshine.
You will always be
in this heart of mine.

A Family that Sleeps Together...

Throughout most of human history, babies and children slept with their moms, or even both parents, in the same bed. This was a pattern determined by the structure of homes—separate sleeping quarters were a luxury most people did not have. It was only two hundred years ago that humans began to build homes with more than one room; even today, many families in the world continue to live in one-room dwellings.

Co-Sleeping

Anthropologist John Whiting has researched sleeping patterns across 136 societies.

- In fully half of these cultures, moms and babies shared a bed while dad slept elsewhere.

- In 16 percent of them, mom and dad and children slept together. Interestingly, this pattern seems to be influenced by climate. Where it is cold, parents and children share a bed, presumably for warmth.

- In total, in 67 percent of world cultures children sleep with other family members.

USA

Babies in the U.S. are routinely placed in their own beds in their own rooms very early. These sleeping arrangements translate into different mothering styles across cultures. American moms, for example, use soothing lullabies, stories, special clothing, and toys to encourage a pattern of sleeping in a separate room.

- By three months of age, 58 percent of American babies are sleeping in their own room.

- By six months, 97 percent sleep in rooms apart from their moms.

Moms in Asia

Single Moms in Japan

Moms in Japan are less likely to tackle motherhood on their own, according to Women's International Network News.

- One percent of all Japanese births were to unwed mothers, a stark contrast to the roughly 30 percent of American births that are to single moms.

Did You Know. . . ?

- It was not until 1999 that the birth control pill became legal in Japan.

- Moms in Japan got some help from an American expert in 1963, the year Benjamin Spock's *Dr. Spock's Baby and Child Care* was translated into Japanese.

Japanese Moms in the New Millennium

- Japanese women have, on average, 1.88 children. Japanese daughters look to their own moms for support in raising their families.

- According to the Second National Survey on Family in Japan, conducted by the National Institute of Population and Social Security Research in Japan, two thirds of married women with married daughters assisted their married daughters with child-bearing and child rearing.

- Forty percent of married women with married daughters

listened to their children's worries and gave advice on their problems.

- Moms in Japan, like moms everywhere, assume the lion's share of child rearing responsibilities.
- Among married women with children under one year of age, 80 percent of child rearing activities are assumed by mom.
- About 10 percent of these new moms get no help from their husbands in these tasks.
- Although 90 percent of married women believe that moms with small kids should concentrate on raising their children, half of all married women in Japan return to work after bearing children.

Traditional Chinese Birth Customs

With such a long history, China is steeped in tradition and superstition. Pregnancy practices are adhered to for all of the obvious medical reasons, but also to protect new moms and babies from "malign influences."

- Hammers and nails are avoided, because they are believed to cause birth defects.
- Expectant moms must curb foul language, because this may cause the baby to be cursed.
- Harming an animal during pregnancy is much frowned upon because of the fear that the baby will be affected. It is believed, for example, that if a pregnant mom strikes a rat, her newborn will look and behave like that rodent.
- Pregnant women are encouraged to work, as this is believed to ease labor and delivery.
- Pregnant moms should also curb arguments and watch her diet: certain "sharp" foods like pineapple are believed to cause birth defects.

- Pregnant moms are advised to resist the urge to rub their growing bellies, as such actions are believed to result in spoiled and demanding children.

- When pregnant, Chinese women avoid working with glue or other adhesives because it is believed that this will cause birth complications.

❧

❧ What Is It?

Chinese moms rarely name a child before it is born. Doing so displays unsavory eagerness on the part of parents for a child of a particular sex, and in Chinese culture male heirs continue to be important.

- Superstitions like eating certain foods in the days leading up to conception are said to influence the sex of the baby. Tofu, mushrooms, carrots, and lettuce guarantee a boy; pickles, meat, and fish, a baby girl.

- After a baby is born, the Chinese are careful not to heap praise on the new baby because it attracts demons and ghosts.

- An "innie" belly button is a sign of a prosperous life.

- A baby's head should be regularly stroked to guarantee it becomes nicely rounded.

- After birth, mom is subject to a forty-day period of confinement, during which time she is to keep warm, eat warm foods, and avoid cold baths.

- About a month after the birth, a small celebration of the new baby is held. The day after the baby's hair is shaved off, an act perceived to encourage further hair growth.

- Babies who cry a lot are said to be disturbed by evil spirits. To ward these off, a single pamelo leaf is placed beneath the baby's mattress.

Draupadi: A Revered Mom in India

Throughout Indian history, women and their roles as wife and mother have been glorified. While the status of a woman was traditionally connected to that of her husband, a woman's position in the household was one of much authority and honor, and no Hindu ceremony was complete without mom. The great Indian epics have highlighted women in these roles; a classic example is the character Draupadi in the epic "Mahabharata". Draupadi was the strong and determined daughter born to King Drupada. She was known for her loveliness, her virtue, her aroma of fresh blooming lotus, and her fiery, strong will.

Though bent on vengeance, Draupadi could also be compassionate, and resolved not to harm good people but to stand firm before the wicked. She married five husbands, strove to accommodate their needs and wishes, and yet in some ways was mistreated by all. Despite her difficulties, she bore five sons, maintained the reputations of her husbands, and honored her parents. Despite her hardships, she wished her husbands to feel they were married to a great woman. Draupadi represents selflessness, and sacrifices her own happiness to give herself fully to her role as wife and mother.

❧

Moms in Israel

Israel is an extremely family-oriented society. This is the result of a couple of factors. First, the family is central in the Jewish tradition that defines Israeli culture. In addition, Israeli recognition of its precariousness and contested existence has made large families, and the demographic stability they bring, an important consideration and an official state goal. Indeed, at one time there was a government department that was responsible for the promotion of large families. In Israel, moms are seen as the "glue" that binds the all-important family together. Women feel great pressure to marry and to carry out this important responsibility.

Like the Ashes and the Hearth

An Aztec woman's life was decided from the moment of her birth. The attending midwife would explain to the screaming newborn girl, "You must live in the house like the heart in the body. You must not leave the house…You must be like the ashes and the hearth." Girls were expected to embrace the hardship that would be her lot in life as a wife and mother.

Aztec girls grew up in their households watching their mom, learning by example. When they turned seven, they began to learn the important duties of a woman, learning to sweep the house, spin cotton, grind corn, and use the loom. Girls were held to a particularly strict code of conduct. Bold behavior was frowned upon, as was talking during meals or addressing a boy. At age fifteen, Aztec girls entered the school system, remarkable for the time. Girls became marriageable at age twenty, and at this point left school to begin life in their own homes. The wedding day was fully six days of feasting, celebration, and ceremony.

Soon after marriage, women were expected to give birth, and pregnancy caused much joy and was celebrated with a banquet. A midwife would be involved in the pregnancy from the beginning. She massaged the expectant mom and bathed her in warm water. As birth neared, the mother was given medicines made of bark and opossum tail for the pain. At the moment of birth, the midwife let out a war cry to honor the mother and greeted the new baby with news of her place as the "ashes and hearth" of Aztec society.

Cross-Cultural Adoption

Chinese Adoption

Americans adopting children cross-culturally is an ever-growing phenomenon.

- In an average month, three-hundred-fifty young girls leave their native China to live with American parents.

- According to the INS, close to 35,000 children from China have been adopted by American families since 1985.

- According to Children's Hope International, the estimated cost of such an adoption (without including travel expenses) is $11,015.00, and the estimated travel costs for two to China, $16,215.00.

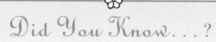

Did You Know . . . ?

In 2003 alone, 21,616 children were adopted through international adoption.

Take Five: The Top Five Countries for Americans' International Adoptions

1. China (6,859 children)
2. Russia (5,209 children)
3. Guatemala (2,328 children)
4. South Korea (2,328 children)
5. Kazakhstan (825 children)

Source: U.S. Dept. Of State, Office of Visa Processing

Australian Aborigines: Rituals of the Warlpiri

There are at least five hundred Aboriginal groups in Australia. The semi-nomadic Warlpiri of the Central Desert of the Northern Territory are one such group. Some Warlpiri live in modern settings, but most live in "fringe" communities that evolved from mission sites of the last century. As such, their lives are infused with religion and ritual, and these beliefs permeate issues of motherhood and birth.

For example, instead of having a sonogram, the Walpiri try to determine which conception spirit caused the pregnancy and thus determine which spiritual identity belongs to the baby. When it comes time for delivery, it is very important that the Walpiri mom deliver onto the ground, as the ground contains the life source needed to sustain the Walpiri people. When the baby is born, the Mom "smokes" her baby over smoking acacia leaves, believing this gives the baby strength.

Held in High Esteem: Infancy in Bali

Bali is one of the 6000 Islands of Indonesia, where 95 percent of the population practices Balinese Hinduism. Central to this faith are the ideas that all acts have consequences and that one's soul is reincarnated after death until a perfect life is attained and one reaches unity with god. This religion profoundly influences Balinese beliefs and practices surrounding birth and motherhood.

A pregnant woman and her husband take precautions to ensure a trouble-free pregnancy. They make frequent offerings to their ancestors and gods to protect the unborn child from evil spirits. Boys are favored because sons and grandsons can one day perform the cremation and purification rites that allow the soul to be liberated at death.

At birth, a baby is considered to be divine and, having just arrived from heaven, is treated as a celestial being. Babies are held high—literally—as those of higher rank are always elevated to their inferiors. Babies are never placed on the floor. Until the otonan ceremony, the baby is always carried. At this ceremony, the child crosses from the divine world to the human world, and his or her feet are placed on the floor for the first time.

Survey Says...

Culture influences the age at which moms in America begin their families, according to AgeVenture News Service. Since 1970, moms in America began to wait longer to have families.

- In 1970, moms were, on average, 24.6 years old when they had their first baby.

- By 2000, this had increased to 27.2 years. Despite these national averages, in the American melting pot, culture continues to have considerable influence on the age at which women in America first give birth.

- American moms of Chinese or Japanese origin are typically older than the national average, at about thirty years of age.

- Cuban-American moms are twenty-seven.

- White Americans are twenty-six.

- Black Americans slightly younger, at twenty-two; also the age at which Hispanic Americans from Puerto Rica and Mexico have their first babies.

- Native American moms are among the youngest at their first birth, at about twenty-one years old.

7

Mothers of the Earth

Original Mothers of the Continent

The first mothers to live in North America were, of course, those of Native American ancestry—but who exactly was the first North American mother? Native Americans maintain their people created North America and they were created on it. Most of the Native American creation stories celebrate strong, powerful, life-giving mother figures.

In these stories it is a female power who creates the Earth and all its creatures. Sometimes this female power has the help of the Great Spirit, who is both male and female. In some of the myths, the people are trapped underground and are searching for their way to the surface. They must travel through several caves (the "wombs" of Mother Earth) before reaching the surface.

Ataensic

The Iroquois believe that Ataensic, the Sky Mother, gave birth to twins—the spirits of good and evil. The good twin was committed to beautifying the earth, while his brother was committed to destroying it.

At their birth, Ataensic died. Grieving the loss of his mother, the good twin created the sun from her face, while the evil twin placed darkness in the western sky, forcing the sun behind it. But Ataensic's importance was not negated. The good twin formed the moon and stars from the breast of his mother to guard the night sky. He then gave the Earth her body, from whence was to spring all life.

Navajo and Apache

The "Changing Woman" is an important Navajo deity, called the mother of the people. The Changing Woman was the first child of the first man and the first woman. Impregnated by her husband, the Sun, Changing Woman became the first woman to physically give birth. She gave birth to twin sons, Monster Slayer and Child of the Water. She is credited with creating the Earth Surface People, the ancestors of the Navajos. Changing Woman had power over reproduction and birth in all of Earth's creation.

Thompson

The creation story of the Thompson Native Americans of the Pacific Northwest stresses the importance of women's power of fertility, and celebrates a mother's sacrifice and unconditional love. According to this story, the earth was originally like a human. She had a head, arms and legs, and an enormous fat belly.

The original human beings lived on the surface of her belly. One day she realized that if she got up and walked about, everyone would fall off and be killed. Rather than subject her "children" to this fate, she killed herself. Her head became the snow-covered mountains, and the bones of her back turned into smaller hills. Her chest was the valley where the Apa-Tanis live. From her neck came the north country of the Tagins. Her buttocks turned into the Assam plain. For just as the buttocks are full of fat, Assam has fat rich soil. Her eyes became the sun and the moon.

In these Native American stories, woman's role as mother to the people was vital to the physical and spiritual well-being of the clan and the tribe. One Dakota elder described the importance of mothers like this: "It is well to be good to women in the strength of our manhood, because we must sit under their hands at both ends of our life."

"In the beginning there was thought, and her name was Woman."
—*Paula Gunn Allen,* The Sacred Hoop

White Buffalo Calf Woman

White Buffalo Calf Woman is part of the creation story of the Lakota. She appeared as a beautiful maiden on the Great Plains, dressed in white buckskin. There she met two Lakota hunters. One of the hunters confided to the other that he lusted after White Buffalo Calf Woman. Recognizing her sacredness, his companion urged the evil-thinker not to think of her in this way. When she approached the two men, White Buffalo Calf Woman looked at the evil man. He was immediately surrounded by clouds. When the cloud dissipated, there remained only a pile of human bones, covered in slithering snakes.

White Buffalo Calf Woman instructed the other hunter to tell his village that the next day she would return with a message from the Great Spirit. The young man did as he was told, and the people erected a tipi in anticipation of her arrival.

When she appeared, she was carrying the first sacred pipe. White Buffalo Calf Woman explained that the stem of the pipe represents man, and the bowl, woman, or the earth. She told the people that whoever prayed with the sacred pipe would be in harmony with the universe.

Quotable Mom

"My dear sisters, the women: you have a hard life to live in this world, yet without you this life would not be what it is. Wakantanka [the Great Spirit] intends that you shall bear much sorrow, and comfort others in time of sorrow. By your hand the family moves. You have been given the knowledge of making clothing and feeding your family. Wakantanka is

with you in your sorrows and joins you in your grief.
He has given you the greatest kindness towards every living
creature on earth. You he has chosen to have a feeling for the dead
who are gone. He knows that you remember the dead longer
than do the men. He knows that you love your children dearly."
—White Buffalo Calf Woman
("Walking in the Sacred Manner," Mark St. Pierre and
Tilda Long Soldier)

Path to Motherhood

Fertility is the most celebrated power of Native women. Many Native American cultures have rituals that celebrate a girl's progression toward motherhood. The first milestone is marked by a girl's first menstrual cycle. An important ceremony accompanies the event.

This ritual is so important that parents of girls start preparing for it when their daughter is only eight or nine years old. At that time, parents ask an old woman to start watching their daughter, protecting her virginity until she is married. During the girl's first menstrual period, the girl is isolated along with other women who are menstruating. When the girl's first menstruation is finished, there is a celebration.

Sunrise

Like many plains people, the Apache celebrate this passage in a woman's life with a sunrise ceremony marked by four events.

- The first, a sweat bath, is held in the morning and attended by male relatives.

- The second is the food exchange, when a gift of prepared food is presented to the relatives of the pubescent girl by her female sponsor.

- The third is a short ceremony at dusk. Accompanied

by her sponsor, the girl is presented with new clothes. The old woman makes a fire of sage and sweet grass and runs the clothes through the smoke to purify them. The woman paints the girl's face red to symbolize her rebirth, and to symbolize the earth itself.

• Part four is a dance where the girl dances in her special costume. Throughout most of na'ii'ees, the girl's power is used to benefit herself. Immediately after the ceremony, her power becomes public property and is available to everyone. At this time she is considered holy and continues to live at the dance ground with her family.

Marriage

In most Native American societies, children married at a relatively young age. Girls were considered eligible for marriage after first menstruation, and boys usually married by age twenty. Although most societies tolerated sexual activity before marriage, some, like the Cheyenne and Crow cultures, highly valued premarital sexual abstinence.

Parents or other older relatives usually chose a mate for their children, and in some tribes, marriages were arranged during a child's early childhood. In other areas, young people had greater say in their choice of spouse and if a boy and girl expressed interest in each other, their families would decide whether to permit them to marry. The only rule that universally governed the choice of marriage partners was a strong taboo against marrying close relatives.

Childbirth

Pregnant women functioned as they always had in their communities. When the time for giving birth arrived, the expectant mother was given a safe and comfortable place to give birth.

Among the Lakota people, soft skins were arranged in a lodge and the woman was instructed to kneel in the center of the lodge, holding a tipi poll for support.

Assisting at birth was the domain only of women who had themselves given birth. Situated at the center of the lodge, the laboring mother received support from female elders who oversaw the birth

Following the birth, these same elders would help the mother deliver the placenta and help cut the umbilical cord. A section of the cord would be saved and placed in a special pouch that was usually made in the shape of a lizard or turtle.

Called "birth amulets," these pouches were believed to offer spiritual protection to the new child. Following birth, new mothers would be anointed with bear grease scented with beaver castor. It was believed that this ceremony would instill in the new baby the strength of a bear and the industry of a beaver—both valuable traits.

Native American Herbal Remedies for Childbirth

- Partridgeberry: The Cherokee used a tea of the boiled leaves. Frequent doses of the tea were taken in the few weeks preceding the expected date of delivery.

- Blue Cohosh: An expectant mom drinks the infusion of the root in warm water as a tea for several weeks prior to the expected delivery date to promote a rapid delivery.

- American Licorice: A tea made from this plant's boiled root is said to speed delivery of the placenta.

- Broom Snakeweed: Navajo women drank a tea of the whole plant to promote the expulsion of the placenta.

- Buckwheat: Hopi women were given an infusion of the entire buckwheat plant to stop post-partum bleeding.

- Black Western Chokecherry: Arikara women were given a drink of the berry juice to stop bleeding.

- Smooth Upland Sumac: The Omahas boiled the smooth upland sumac fruits and applied the liquid as an external wash to stop bleeding.

- Wild Black Cherry. Cherokee women were given a tea of the inner bark to relieve pain in the early stages of childbirth.

- Cotton: The Alabama and Koasati tribes made a tea of the roots of the plant to relieve the pains of labor.

- Ragleaf Bahia: The Navajos, who called the ragleaf bahia herb "twisted medicine", drank a tea of the roots boiled in water for thirty minutes for contraception purposes.

- Indian Paintbrush: Hopi women drank a tea of the whole Indian paintbrush to "dry up the menstrual flow."

- Blue Cohosh: Chippewa women drank a strong decoction of the powdered blue cohosh root to promote parturition and menstruation.

- Dogbane: Generally used by many tribes, a tea from the boiled roots of the plant was drunk once a week to avoid conception.

- Milkweed: Navajo women drank a tea prepared of the whole plant after childbirth.

- American Mistletoe: Indians of Mendocino County drank a tea of the leaves to induce abortion or to prevent conception.

- Antelope Sage: To prevent conception, Navajo women drank one cup of a decoction of boiled antelope sage root during menstruation.

- Stoneseed: Shoshoni women of Nevada reportedly drank a cold water infusion of stoneseed roots everyday for six months to ensure permanent sterility.

New Moms

After giving birth, new mothers were given special herb teas and on the prairies, a broth made from buffalo meat. They did not immediately nurse their babies as the first milk was believed to be unhealthy. Instead, a well-respected elder was invited (and highly honored) to nourish new babies. Lakotas placed leather caps decorated with quill work on the head of newborn babies. This would offer protection and also encourage the proper closing of the child's fontanel.

Huggies

Tribes used various absorbent substances—such as moss—for "diapers." Infants born to Native cultures across the continent were swaddled on cradle boards—contraptions that not only quieted fussy babies but that also allowed a mother the freedom to fulfill her day-to-day duties. After the child had been placed in a cradle board, it would be presented to its father.

Named After

Parents did not name their child—rather the honor of choosing a name was left to a respected couple who would present their name choice in a public ceremony and celebration that formally welcomed the baby into the community. The birth of babies was a time of celebration; the arrival of a new community member was associated with the mystery of life and death and served to remind people of just how closely connected people were to the spirit world.

Native American Child Rearing

Child rearing in Native societies differed markedly from that of Europe. While European parents tended to direct children verbally, Native parents allowed children to learn through their own observations. By observing, praying, dancing, and chanting, children were taught at a very early age the importance and power of the spirit world. Native children were excluded from no aspects of life. In many societies children were believed to be reincarnated ancestors who, if ill-treated, would leave the community.

It Takes a Village

In her 1996 book *It Takes a Village*, Senator Hillary Clinton espoused a child-rearing philosophy that urged all Americans to take collective responsibility in the nurturing and raising of children. This was a concept that Native Americans knew well. Children were raised in an extensive kinship system that tied all people to one another. All adults shared in child-raising responsibilities.

Grandparents were especially important. As elders, their wisdom was deemed to be of much importance to the next generation, and grandparents and grandchildren had a close bond. In such fluid family networks, adoption was not uncommon. Children sometimes were sent to live with non-parent relatives, or were given to families who had lost children. Adoptees were accepted by their new families completely, just as if they had been born to them.

Birth Control

In Native American societies it was not uncommon for children to be nursed for five, even six years. While this practice might serve to ease times of famine, it is also likely that this was a tactic used to postpone pregnancy, as women who are nursing are less likely to become pregnant.

NANCY WARD (CA. 1738-CA. 1824)

Nan'yehi, aka Nancy Ward, was born in 1738—at a time of much turmoil for her Cherokee people. She was raised by her mother, Tame Deer, and her father, Fivekiller. At that time, Christian missionaries were seeking to change Cherokee culture, and the Cherokee were divided. Some saw Christianity as a threat, others saw it as a blessing. Raised in a time of such conflict, Nan'yehi learned to seek middle ground between tradition and innovation.

In her early teens, she married a great warrior, Kingfisher. In 1755, when she was just eighteen, Kingfisher was killed in battle, leaving her a widow with three children. Nan'yehi took her slain husband's gun and lead her people to victory in the Battle of Taliwa. Such bravery earned her the respect of her people and the name "Beloved Woman."

BELOVED WOMAN

Her prestige gave Nan'yehi a lifetime voice in tribal councils, as well as the power to pardon condemned captives. This privilege was unprecedented in the Cherokee culture. Nan'yehi used her power to serve as a peace negotiator, a skill that had been ingrained in her as a young girl. She discouraged senseless killings, but also refused to counsel peace if she felt it would compromise her tribe. In 1785, she negotiated the Cherokee's first treaty with the United States.

In later years, she married Bryant Ward, and together they ran an inn. The prestige that Ward earned among her people was virtually unimaginable for non-Native women of the eighteenth century. In 1824, Ward returned to the place of her birth, and her son, Fivekiller, cared for her until her death that same year. She was the last woman to be given the title of "Beloved Woman" until the late 1980s.

Raising the Three Sisters

The most widely known example of female-centered horticulture is that of the "Three Sisters" in the Northeast. These are corn, beans, and squash—the mainstays for most nations in the Americas. Planted and harvested by women, the Three Sisters emerge from the womb of mother earth to provide food for the people. In addition to planting, nurturing and harvesting the Three Sisters, women performed other horticultural activities, which included maintaining knowledge of herbs and their uses in both medicinal and culinary arts.

Quotable Mom

"She is the mother of all, in fertility, in holding, in taking us again back to her breast." —Keres ceremonial prayer

Trail of Tears: Legend of the Cherokee Rose

In 1838 President Andrew Jackson authorized the removal of thousands of Cherokee from their homeland to "Indian Territory." The now infamous Trail of Tears is one of the most tragic chapters in American history.

During a winter noted for its brutality, thousands of men, women and children were forced to march west. Four thousand Cherokee lost their lives. The Cherokee called the removal "Nunna daul Tsuny," literally translated as "The Trail Where They Cried." The Trail of Tears is symbolized by the Cherokee Rose. It is said that the mothers of the Cherokee grieved the loss of their families and homeland so much that their chiefs prayed for a sign to lift their spirits and to give them the strength they needed to care for their children.

According to legend, from that awful day forward, a beautiful rose grew wherever a mother's tear hit the ground. The white of the rose symbolizes the mother's tears while the flower's gold center stands for the gold taken from Cherokee land by white men. The seven leaves on the stem of each rose denote the seven Cherokee clans forced to make the tragic journey. To this day, Cherokee Roses bloom along the Trail of Tears. It is now the official state flower of Georgia.

*"The Great Spirit is in all things, he is in the air we breathe.
The Great Spirit is our Father, but the Earth is our Mother. She
nourishes us; that which we put into the ground she returns to us."*
—Big Thunder (Bedagi)

Mother by Another Name:
Native American Words for "Mother"

Hiaki: ae/maala
O'odham: jeej
Plains Cree: Nikawiy
Haida: díi aw
Potawatomi: ne'ni
Yupik: Aana

You Could Say, We Fell from the Sky

According to Iroquois legend, the human race began as a result
of an unfortunate accident. Skywoman was one day walking
around in the Land Above the Sky when she suddenly fell
through a hole left by an uprooted tree. As she fell, a flock of
geese broke her fall and she landed on a giant turtle that rose up
out of the waters. The giant turtle grew in shape, forming the
land, and it was there that Skywoman gave birth to a daughter
whose children propagated the human race.

First Man, First Woman

According to Navajo legend, the first man and woman ascended
from the underworld together with Coyote, having to lead their
people through many struggles to reach the surface world, which
finally became their first home. This couple had to work
together, though. Deciding that the sky was too empty with only

Sun and Moon, First Man and First Woman gathered up all the glittering stones they could find and placed them in the sky to serve as stars.

In Cherokee legend, Selu, sometimes known as First Woman, created corn in secret by rubbing her belly or by…um…defecating. Her sons, the Twin Thunder Boys, killed her when they caught her in the act, though, taking her for a witch.

8

Mothers on Screen, Stage, Page, and Canvas

"Grown don't mean nothing to a mother. A child is a child. They get bigger, and older, but grown? In my heart it don't mean a thing." —Toni Morrison

Television Moms: The Early Years

Since the 1950s, when the television first became the focal point of American living rooms, the "TV Mom" has reflected back to us a vision of who we are at certain points in time. Watching how mom has evolved since the days of rabbit ears and black-and-white programming in many cases is a map of your own journey, or that of your mother or grandmother.

The theme of many early television shows featuring family life was—as the title of one popular series made perfectly clear—that *Father Knows Best*. In that 1950s series, Jane Wyatt played Margaret Nelson, the wife of an insurance salesman. Don't let the title fool you though; father may have thought he knew best, and even that was debatable, but what was clear in this series was that mother was the steadfast bedrock of home-life.

Picture Perfect Mom

This idea—that the mother is the anchor of the home—runs through many of the popular shows of the 1950s and 1960s. On *I Love Lucy*, a show in which Lucille Ball's real life pregnancy was incorporated into the story line, one of the running gags was that Lucy wished to join her husband Ricky's band. The obvious (and ironic) joke was that show business was no place for a woman or a mother. Still, Lucy was one of TV's first moms to look for happiness (and a career) outside the home.

Another common theme for moms on early television shows was they always had to look presentable. Consider, for example, June Cleaver, the Beaver's famous mother on *Leave it to Beaver*. She did such strange things as baking cookies and cleaning the house while wearing pearls. Really, how many real life moms today would don formal dress to bake?

One thing that was kept off the airwaves during the 1950s and early 1960s was divorce. Almost every family on the tube was a nuclear family. Dad was out earning money while mom stayed home to look after the kids and house. In the event that a non-traditional single parent family did find airtime, the family was almost invariably one that had been broken up by death. Widows and widowers were ok, divorcees were not. And it wasn't until the late 1960s that the historic meeting of a TV widow and widower occurred.

Mom's Getting Cool

In 1969, a "lovely lady" who was bringing up three very lovely girls finds a "man named Brady" who had three boys of his own. They meet, fall in love, and get married. And that's how they became The Brady Bunch. *The Brady Bunch* showed that even in the face of the death of a spouse, the family could thrive. And although Carol Brady's clothing was a lot groovier than that of television moms before her, she was very much a TV mom of the 1950s and 1960s. But unlike the television moms of the '50s, Carol had an assistant. Alice, the Brady's lovable maid, who handled all the domestic chores! What mom wouldn't love that?

Shirley Partridge was another funky 1960s mom. Like *The Brady Bunch's* Carol, Shirley Partridge was a widow. But unlike Carol, Shirley didn't remarry and *The Partridge Family* was one of the first television shows to prominently feature a single mom. And what a fun single mom she was! She took her musical kids on tour with her in their converted school bus (which featured the sign "Caution: Nervous Mother Driving") and the family had all sorts of crazy adventures. But beneath her hip exterior, Shirley Partridge was similar to the other moms on television. She loved her kids, protected them, and wanted nothing but the best for them.

Celebrities on Moms and Motherhood

*"While I prefer not to be like my mother as an actress,
I do honestly aspire to be like her in real life. She's absolutely
unflappable—with a delightful sense of humor."*
—Gwyneth Paltrow ❀

*"It's like you grow another head, like someone kicks down a
door that was sealed shut, and then the whole world—
sunshine, flowers—falls through. I have such joy that
I did not think was possible."*
❀
—Rosie O'Donnell

*"There is nothing more thrilling in this world, I think, than having
a child that is yours, and yet is mysteriously a stranger."*
—Agatha Christie ❀

"I've seen my name in letters as tall as a house.
I've been toasted by audiences who've seen me on international
television. I've won virtually every award my career offers.
I say all that simply to say this: I've never been as fulfilled
as I was when my son was born."
—Reba McEntire

"I've always been amazed by the miracle of it all. And the mystery."
—Christie Brinkley

"This little soul really wants to be here, so it's meant to be."
—Susan Sarandon

"Being a mother is another life. You're at home and you're with
your child, playing with the toys, changing diapers. Life becomes
all about the real stuff; and the rest isn't as important. But don't get
me wrong: to come back and do a record was more fun than ever
because I've never felt as strong. I feel like a complete person."
—Celine Dion

"It's hard to have a dark mood with a gurgling, delightful,
cherubic baby kissing you and hugging you."
—Jane Seymour

"I still love making movies, but I take more pride in
my role as a mother and a wife."
—Michelle Pfeiffer

"Motherhood is the greatest thing I've ever done.
This is the greatest thing I'll ever do."
—Kim Basinger

"My first job is to be a good mother."
—Faye Dunaway

TV Trivia

- Mother Jane Jetson's voice for *The Jetsons* was provided by Penny Singleton, while Jean Vander Pyl portrayed mama Wilma Flintstone in *The Flintstones*.

- Lucy gave birth to Little Ricky during the January 19, 1953, episode of *I Love Lucy*. Lucille Ball gave birth to son Desi Arnaz IV on the exact same day.

- The first televised birth was on December 2, 1952, by KOA in Denver. Lillian Kerr had a Cesarean section as part of the *March of Medicine* program.

- The stereotypical mom June Cleaver first appeared in households in *Leave it to Beaver* on October 4, 1957.

Did You Know...?

Olive May Osmond is the mother of musical siblings made famous by *The Osmond Family Show*. The performing brothers and one sister include: Donnie, Marie, Alan, Wayne, Jay, Merrill, and Jimmy. Donnie and Marie also had their own show.

Take Five: Top Five TV Moms of All Time

1. Marion Cunningham from *Happy Days*
2. Roseanne Conner from *Roseanne*
3. Laura Petrie from *The Dick Van Dyke Show*
4. Murphy Brown from *Murphy Brown*
5. Morticia Addams from *The Addams Family*

Source: E online.

PERFECT MOM: JUNE CLEAVER

The quintessential television mom, June Cleaver, was born June Evelyn Bronson. Her childhood was spent in East St. Louis where she attended boarding school. She later moved to Mayfield as a teenager and attended state college.

When she finished her education, young June Bronson married Ward Cleaver and began what was the most famous suburban lifestyle of her generation. With perpetually fresh coffee, a full cookie jar, and warm pies to spare, June Cleaver managed to tend to husband, children, and house. As Eddie Haskell commented, "…your kitchen always looks so clean. It looks as though you never do any work in here."

In dealing with the messes that her sons Wally and the Beav created, June was always gentle, even-tempered, and fair. Mrs. Cleaver represented an idealized, purified vision of the American family. She represented peace, prosperity, and homogeneity in the suburbs of the nation's cities. Testimony to her enduring power, June Cleaver remains the stereotype of perfect motherhood.

Television Moms of the 1970s

While the 1970s saw TV moms such as *Happy Days'* Mrs. Cunningham, who was apparently the only woman who could make The Fonz nervous, and *All in the Family's* Edith Bunker, who was apparently the only woman who could keep Archie in line, many programs popular during the decade attempted to deal with the issue of single parenthood.

On the popular *Good Times*, Florida Evans (Esther Rolle) was not initially a widow. When the series premiered she was hitched to hubby James, played by actor John Amos of *Roots* fame. But when producers decided that Amos was a disruptive influence, they had him written out of the show by having his character die in a car accident.

This also fit into CBS executives' master plan. They had

originally wanted the show to be about a single mom. It was only by Rolle's insistence that the Evans began as a two-parent family. But with James' death, Florida Evans was left to face the challenge of raising two kids on her own. And despite facing some troubles with drugs and violence, Florida does a good job. On the final episode of

Quotable Mom

"Suddenly she was here. And I was no longer pregnant; I was a mother. I never believed in miracles before."
—*Ellen Greene, actress*

Good Times, Evans' oldest son, J.J., finally fulfills his dream of becoming a successful comic strip writer. Dyn-o-mite!

Single Mom

Another 1970s single mom was Alice Hyatt, title character of the hit sitcom *Alice*. Alice also had lost her husband and had decided to move from New Jersey to Phoenix to follow her dream of becoming a country-and-western singer. The dream proves hard to realize, so Alice takes a job at Mel's Diner—a place where the food looked as unappetizing as the cook—in order to pay her bills and support her son.

Over the years Alice brings up little Tommy with the help of diner owner Mel, and her waitress coworkers, timid Vera and flirtatious Flo. Dreams do come true in the end for Alice. As the series came to a close, Alice moved to Nashville to be the lead singer in a country-and-western band.

One Day

But not all single moms on TV during the '70s were widows. Reflecting the fact that divorce was becoming more common and less stigmatized, *One Day at a Time* introduced Ann Romano Royer (Bonnie Franklin), an Indianapolis divorcee raising two teenage daughters. Most shows focused on the Romano's travails bringing up young Julie (Mackenzie Phillips) and Barbara (Valerie Bertinelli). But the show also examined the Romano family's relationship with a number of father figures.

The most notable of these surrogate dads was the lovable super, Dwayne Schneider, who could always be counted on to help the Romano clan. Other father figures were found in Romano's many love interests, including David, Nick, and eventual husband Sam. She worked hard to support her two kids, bring up two beautiful and well-adjusted daughters, and still found the time to lead an active social life of her own.

> ## Did You Know...?
> *The hit sitcom* Alice *was based on the Oscar-winning movie* ❀ Alice Doesn't Live Here Anymore.

Take Five: Five Single Celebrity Moms

1. Demi Moore ❀

The proud momma of Rumor, Scout, and Tallulah, with ex-hubby Bruce Willis, the buxom Moore has been linked to young heartthrob Ashton Kutcher. Must be tough raising four children alone!

2. Elizabeth Hurley

Star of the *Austin Powers* movies and the ex of Hugh Grant, Hurley has a son named Damian Charles. Hurley contended that real estate heir Steven Bing is the father, although Bing denied paternity. In response, Hurley said "In that case, I'm not sure I'm the mother." DNA testing later proved that Bing was indeed Damian's daddy.

3. Calista Flockhart

The former star of *Ally McBeal* adopted Liam, a son, in January 2000. Said Flockhart of the experience, "It's the best thing that I have done in my life and it really changes who you are. It changes your heart. It's made me tolerant of things I wasn't tolerant of before. It's a miracle. Anybody who has children talks like this, so I'm not unique and I am not special, but I am in love with my child in a way that I have truly never been in love before."

4. Jodie Foster

According to many reports in the British press, this two-time Oscar winner had herself artificially inseminated with the sperm of a tall, dark and handsome scientist with a 160 IQ in order to have the perfect baby. Whether the story is true or not, Foster has two wonderful sons: Charles and Kit. Foster has stated that anyone who wants to know the identity of either of her son's fathers should just ask the boys—when they turn eighteen.

5. Diane Keaton

Although she wasn't a good mother on the big screen, Diane Keaton certainly is one in real life. At forty-nine, an age when many women are contemplating becoming grandmothers, Keaton had her first child, a boy named Dexter. Five years later she did it again, having another boy named Duke. Said Keaton about becoming a mother, "Motherhood has completely changed me. It's just about the most completely humbling experience that I've ever had."

Mob Mom

Livia Soprano was one of the few characters on the TV show *The Sopranos* that could make tough-guy and mob-boss Tony

Soprano wilt. Tony's tough-guy exterior was no match for Livia, a passive-aggressive complainer who was shrewder than anyone cared to believe. While hospitalized, Livia used her hospital room as a base from which she plotted the demise of her son. Tony solved his maternal woes by shipping his mother off to Arizona and just when he suspected that she might "rat him out" to the federal government, she died. Upon shipping her off, Tony sighed, "At last—all my enemies are smoked."

Quotable Mom

"Having a child has made me a lot more sensitive, more responsible, a lot more aware of my actions and my words…I was much more selfish and self-involved before." —Madonna

Did You Know…?

- Wilma Flintstone (nee Slaghoople) first appeared on television on September 30, 1960.

- Wilma was married to Fred, had one daughter Pebbles and two pets: a snorkasaurus named Dino and a sabertooth tiger named Baby Puss.

- Pebbles (Flintstone) was born at the Rockville Hospital on February 22, 10,000 BC at 8:00 p.m. She weighed 6 pounds, 12 ounces.

Television Moms of the 1980s: Arrival of Supermom

Although *Kate and Allie* was an early 1980s hit, these moms were about to be replaced by a series of "supermoms." On the hit sitcom *The Cosby Show*, for example, Cliff Huxtable (Bill Cosby) and his wife Clair (Phylicia Rashad) were a pair of professionals raising five children in an upscale New York neighborhood.

Cliff was a successful doctor who had a practice in the basement, while Clair was a respected attorney.

Despite having such a time-consuming occupation, Clair, with Cliff's help, managed to raise Sondra, Theo, Denise, Vanessa, and Ruby into successful young adults. Sondra ended up going to prestigious Princeton University, while Denise attended the fictitious Hillman College. Clair Huxtable was a mom who could do it all—except make Cliff take off those awful sweaters.

Growing Pains

On *Growing Pains*, Alan Thicke played Jason Seaver, a Long Island psychiatrist who practiced out of his home. His wife Maggie (Joanna Kerns) was a newspaperwoman and then television show anchor who worked in the city. Despite the demands put on her by her successful career, Maggie still found time to be there for her kids. Together with Jason, she raised four children: Mike, Carol, Ben, and Chrissy. They even had time to take in a homeless boy during their last season: Luke Bower was played by a young actor named Leonardo DiCaprio.

Alex Keaton's Mom

Another 1980s television mom who could do it all was *Family Ties'* Elyse Keaton. This was a generation gap comedy in reverse. Elyse and her husband Steven were aging hippies with liberal values, while the main child character, Alex P. Keaton (Michael J. Fox), was a reflection of Reagan-era conservative values, even going so far as to sleep with a picture of William F. Buckley, Jr. over his bed. In fact, President Reagan even stated once that *Family Ties* was his favorite television show!

Like *The Cosby Show* and *Growing Pains*, this program also featured a pair of professional parents. But unlike those other two shows, where the primary breadwinner was never certain, on *Family Ties* it was clear that architect mom Elyse brought home more bacon than her public television station managing husband. But Elyse managed to juggle the demands of career and home, and ensured that the Keaton household was a loving one.

Another television show that featured a mom as the primary money earner was *Who's the Boss*. On this hit show, injury forced big league baseball player Tony Micelli (Tony Danza) to retire from the game. Micelli then does what any former major leaguer would do—he packs up his daughter Samantha and moves to Connecticut to be housekeeper for a successful single advertising woman! While Angela dazzles the business world, her home is anything but dazzling, and she needs Tony's domestic help. So Angela brings home the big bucks, while Tony stays home to cook, clean, and look after the kids.

Did You Know...?

That the original title for the pilot script of Kate and Allie *was* Two Mommies?

Take Five: Five Funny Moms

1. Roseanne Barr

As the acerbic mother on the hit sitcom *Roseanne*, Barr raised three strange (and strangely normal) kids. That's one less than Barr has in real life. The sitcom star has three children from an early marriage and one with Ben Thomas.

2. Patricia Heaton

This *Everybody Loves Raymond* funny lady has four little boys with her husband, British actor David Hunt.

3. Jane Leeves

Leeves is better known to TV viewers as Daphne, the Manchester-born caregiver to Dr. Frasier Crain's father on the hit series *Frasier*. She has been married to Marshall Coben, whom she met at a *Frasier* Christmas party, since 1996, and has two young children named Isabella and Finn.

4. Lisa Kudrow

This Vassar-educated actress played the ditsy Phoebe on the hit sitcom *Friends*. On that show, Phoebe was a surrogate mother for her brother and his wife. In real life, Emmy-winning Kudrow has a son, Julian, with husband Michael Stern.

5. Rosie O'Donnell

This stand-up star and former talk show host has three adopted children: Parker, Chelsea and Blake.

The Truth about Mother Goose

Mother Goose is the moniker used to identify the countless anonymous women who have sung for young children throughout history. Mothers, daughters, aunts, grandmothers, sisters, nursemaids, and nannies, each have handed down songs to children in the folk tradition. Debate continues regarding the historical identity of the original Mother Goose (or *La Mere Oie*).

If there is indeed a "real" Mother Goose, she could well have been the eighth-century noblewoman Bertrand II of Laon. Bertrand was married to Pepin the Short, "King of the Franks." She bore a son Charles, the man who would become Charlemagne, Holy Roman Emperor.

Bertrand was a patroness of children, and this might explain her connection to children's stories. In the end, the "real" Mother Goose remains elusive. While some commentators claim that Mother Goose was a clever political satirist, her greatest gift may have been to human development.

Song Science

Today, scientists are exploring the nature of music and its amazing effects on brain development. Songs and lullabies appear to be vital to child development. Through simple songs and rhymes, babies learn to speak and read, to think and make connections. The nature of music brings order to their little lives and helps them develop trust and compassion for others. Songs carry culture and an understanding of humanity.

Though historically women may have been unaware of the science behind songs and child development, they instinctively delivered to children this essential human expression and offered the world their collective maternal wisdom. The collected songs, stories, and rhymes may be credited to Mother Goose, but in that name is the identity of the countless women who have raised successive generations of children around the globe.

Take Five: Top Five Worst Country and Western Song Titles about Mom

1. "Don't Chop Any Wood Mother, I'm Coming With a Load"
2. "I'm the Only Hell My Momma Ever Raised"
3. "Mama Get the Hammer (There's a Fly on Papa's Head)"
4. "Mommy, Can I Still Call Him Daddy?"
5. "Saddle Up the Stove Ma, I'm Riding the Range Tonight"

Source: DownStream Pictures

Take Five: Five Musical Moms

1. Madonna

No list of the top five musical moms would be complete without the Material Girl. Madonna is mommy to Lourdes and Rocco. She is married to British film director Guy Ritchie.

2. Lauryn Hill

Although Lauryn Hill was one third of the successful rap group The Fugees, it wasn't until she branched out on her own that she achieved true critical acclaim. Her 1999 smash recording, *The Miseducation of Lauryn Hill*, was on numerous top ten lists, and won the Grammy for best album. Hill has four children with ex-football player Rohan Marley, son of reggae legend Bob Marley.

3. Celine Dion

Celine Dion is no stranger to the top of the charts. This French-Canadian born superstar is currently playing a running gig in Las Vegas. She has one son, Rene Charles, with her manager/husband, Rene.

4. Shania Twain

Country music superstar Shania Twain is the biggest selling solo female artist in music history. Her 1999 album *Come on Over* sold over 34 million copies on its own! She has a son, Aja, with husband Mutt Lange, a well-known record producer.

5. Courtney Love

Remember, this is five Musical Moms—not the five best Musical Moms. Courtney Love, lead singer of the now defunct grunge-rock group Hole, has a daughter named Frances Bean by her late husband, rock legend Kurt Cobain. Love's reported substance abuse problems have led to trouble with the authorities over custody of Frances. (That's why we're listing Courtney last!)

Writer, poet, performer, director, and mother, Maya Angelou was born Marguerite Johnson on April 4, 1928, in St. Louis, Missouri. After her parents' divorce, Angelou and her older brother, who gave her the nickname "Maya," moved to Stamps, Arkansas to live with their paternal grandmother. In 1940, she moved again, this time to San Francisco to live with her mother. It was here Angelou won a scholarship in dance and drama to the California Labor School. In 1945, just after graduation, her son, Clyde "Guy" Johnson, was born. In the early 1950s, Angelou was married for three years to a former sailor, Tosh Angelos, and she took a variation of his name as her stage name.

NEW YORK CITY

Angelou moved to New York in the late 1950s to pursue her acting and singing careers, appearing in an off-Broadway play *Calypso Heatwave* (1957) and recording an album of calypso music. In 1960, Angelou wrote a revue called *Freedom Cabaret*, which she and her friend Godfrey Cambridge produced, directed, and starred in, in order to raise money for Martin Luther King Jr.'s Southern Christian Leadership Conference (SCLC).

She became the northern coordinator of the SCLC in 1961. Angelou later moved to Egypt with her new husband but that marriage ended in 1963. Angelou then moved to Ghana, where her son was attending college. There, she worked as a teacher and editor for the *African Review* and the *Ghanaian Times*. She returned to Los Angeles in 1966, where she wrote a play, *The Least of These*, and a television series, *Black, Blues, Black*, that dealt with the role of African culture in American life.

WHAT A DEBUT

Encouraged by prominent writers to write the story of her own life in the same powerful style in which she performed, Angelou published her first book, *I Know Why the Caged Bird Sings*, in 1970. The story of her life until the birth of her son, the memoir met with astonishing critical acclaim and popular success. Her performing career also continued on Broadway in *Look Away* (1975), for which she was nominated for a Tony Award, and on TV, in the hugely popular 1977 TV miniseries *Roots*.

Angelou also gained worldwide renown as a poet. She was nominated for a Pulitzer Prize in 1971 for her first volume of verse, entitled *Just Give Me a Cool Drink of Water 'fore I Diiie*. In January 1993, Angelou became the first poet since Robert Frost (in 1961) to take part in a presidential inauguration ceremony when she wrote and read "On the Pulse of Morning," at President Bill Clinton's inauguration. Angelou has since moved to Winston-Salem, and has a great-granddaughter, Caylin Johnson, born in February 1998. ❁

THE PERSISTENT MOM OF A LITERARY GENIUS

In 1976, while a teacher at Loyola University, Walter Percy ❁ began to receive harried phone calls from Thelma Toole. Toole was adamant that Percy read a novel manuscript—one written during the 1960s by her son who, tragically, had recently committed suicide. Percy was doubtful about reading the dead man's book, but tenacious Thelma was persuasive, and Percy reluctantly agreed.

As he read the manuscript he was amazed. The book was not just good, it was incredibly good. Not only did the novel end up getting published, it won one of the literary world's most prestigious awards. Thanks to the efforts of his mom, John Kennedy Toole won the 1981 Pulitzer Prize posthumously for his now classic comic novel *A Confederacy of Dunces*. A book reviewer for the magazine *New Republic* described Toole's novel as "one of the funniest books ever written."

Mom with Pride and Prejudice

Mrs. Bennet is perhaps Jane Austen's greatest gossip and most audacious mother character. Mrs. Bennet is a discontented, stay-at-home wife and mother who was described as a "woman of mean understanding, little information, and uncertain temper" whose "business is to get her daughters married." Austen's work is full of examples of Mrs. Bennet's "ignorance and folly" as well as her quirks—her love of hats, dresses, and balls, and her utter love of young men in uniform.

Sethe: A Tragic Literary Mom

In her gripping best-selling novel *Beloved*, Toni Morrison depicts the love of a mother for her child and the dehumanizing aspects of slavery. Having fled slavery with her children, Sethe finds the slave master on her trail and is desperate to escape him.

Best Little Mom on the Prairie

One of the most endearing moms in America is Caroline "Ma" Ingalls, the quiet, wise, and loving matriarch of the *Little House on the Prairie* book series and the TV show of the same name. In real life, Caroline Lake Quiner was born on December 12, 1839 in Wisconsin. Her life, like that of so many pioneers, was not an easy one. When she was five years old, Caroline's father died, and for the next five years her mother was left to raise their seven children alone.

Caroline took one of the few jobs open to women when she became a school teacher at age 16. On February 1, 1860, she married Charles Ingalls. Together, they had five children, including four surviving girls and a boy who died in infancy.

Gentle and hardworking, Ma did her best to raise her young girls as ladies in the wild west. Somehow she always managed to make ends meet. Caroline had a profound impact on her children. Her most famous child, Laura Ingalls Wilder, was certainly proud of her mom, and Caroline emerges from the pages of Wilder's Little House books as a woman of many talents—an expert seamstress, gardener, and cook—and a woman of profound quiet wisdom. Caroline died on Easter Sunday, 1924.

LUCILLE BALL

Born on August 6, 1911, Lucille Desiree Ball grew up to be one of the most famous and innovative actresses, comediennes and producers in entertainment history. Lucille recognized her calling at an early age and in 1934 landed her first movie role. By the late 1940s, she had appeared in more than sixty films. A celebrated mom in real life, Lucille's work revolutionized America's expectations of the TV mom.

In 1940, Lucille met, fell in love with, and wed her co-star, Cuban bandleader Desi Arnez. When their marriage got off to a rocky start, the oft-separated Desi and Lucille decided to spend more time working together. In 1944, the couple pitched a show to CBS—a situation comedy featuring the marital antics of a fiery redhead and her Cuban bandleader husband. When the network passed on the idea, the couple funded their own pilot of *I Love Lucy*. Newly convinced of its merit, CBS picked it up and *I Love Lucy* became a smash hit. In its sixth year, 179 episode run, it garnered a total of five Emmys.

NEW ERA
The program pushed the limits of acceptable television content. *I Love Lucy* brought the taboo subjects of pregnancy and birth into Americans' living rooms. In a plot line never before seen on

TV, Lucille's real-life pregnancy with her first child, Desi Jr., became part of the *I Love Lucy* story. It must have been a shock to 44 million viewers who watched in January 1953 as Lucy gave birth to "Little Ricky." Following the birth of their real life son, Lucille and Desi's relationship teetered again and they pulled the plug on *I Love Lucy*.

In 1960, their twenty-year marriage ended in divorce. Lucy, however, continued to parlay her motherhood TV success with a six year solo run of *The Lucy Show*, featuring her real life children Desi Jr. and Lucie. A third successful program, *Here's Lucy*, was followed by cinematic success for Ball. She also sat at the helm of her own production company. On April 26, 1989 just weeks after her final small screen appearance at the 1989 Academy Awards, Lucille Ball died of complications following open-heart surgery.

Did You Know...?

In 1907, Russian writer Maxim Gorky penned "Mother," later considered the first work of socialist realism.

Take Five: Top Five TV Moms Americans Want as Their Own

1. Clair Huxtable, *The Cosby Show*
2. Marion Cunningham, *Happy Days*
3. Caroline Ingalls, *Little House on the Prairie*
4. June Cleaver, *Leave it to Beaver*
5. Roseanne Barr, *Rosanne!* & Marge Simpson, *The Simpsons* (tie)

Source: The Home Town Channel.com

Television Moms of the 1990s and Beyond

The supermom trend of the 1980s didn't die with the dawn of a new decade. One notable supermom on the airwaves was *Murphy Brown*, but Brown's foray into parenthood did not occur without controversy. In 1992, Candice Bergen's title character got pregnant. And although she had her choice of two suitors, her ex-husband, Jake, and a more recent boyfriend, Jerry, Brown decided to raise the baby on her own.

This was too much for Vice President Dan Quayle. In a speech, the then vice president derided Bergen's character for "mocking the importance of fathers by bearing a child alone and calling it just another lifestyle choice."

Rosie

The 1990s saw a shift in the way mothers were portrayed on television. On the hit sitcom *Roseanne*, title character Roseanne Conner (Roseanne Barr) was a woman who married her high-school sweetheart Dan (John Goodman), and settled down to a blue-collared life in Illinois. She and Dan worked a series of jobs they hated in order to provide for their three kids, Becky, Darlene, and D.J.

Roseanne was unlike most mothers we had seen on television before. She was a mom who didn't cook (or cook well, with the notable exception of the meat sandwich—a talent she translated into a successful restaurant venture). But although Roseanne didn't have all the answers, she was always there for her kids.

Married With...

The same can't be said for Peg Bundy, matriarch of the Bundy clan on *Married With Children*. Peg and her tall bouffant of red hair stayed at home while her husband Al tried to support the family on his shoe salesman's salary. Peg certainly couldn't be described as a homemaker, because she quite proudly didn't deign to do housework. Despite the fact that neither Peg nor Al (nor either of children) ever raised a finger to clean the home, it never seemed to get too dirty. Like Roseanne, Peg didn't have all the answers; unlike Roseanne, though, Peg didn't seem to care. Peg Bundy wasn't a supermom; she was a super bad mom.

❀

Super Marge

Like Peg Bundy, the 1990s most recognizable television mom also had a tall bouffant of hair. Unlike Peg, Marge Simpson's hair was blue, her skin was yellow, and she cared about her house and home. On the hit cartoon series *The Simpsons*, Marge is the wife of an overweight nuclear power plant employee, Homer, and mother to three young children—loveable under-achiever Bart, loveable overachiever Lisa, and baby Maggy. Marge was always able to keep her family on track and ensure that the two men in her life did the right thing.

Although she was essentially a stay-at-home mom, Marge occasionally entered the workforce. In one episode she joined the police force. But her stay on the force was short-lived, for despite being the finest cop in the Springfield Police Department, the strain of the job proved too much for the family, and she returned to the homestead. For Marge, family always comes first.

Marge Simpson is without question the glue that holds together what is most likely television's most dysfunctional family. And now, finally, she is getting the respect she deserves. The beset mother was recently named Most Idolized Role Model in a survey by Britain's Mother's Union. She may be an obsessive-compulsive cleaner wed to an oaf and mother to a juvenile delinquent and a politically correct nag, but Marge rarely loses her cool, preferring to express her displeasure through her signature groan. Marge always comes across as good-hearted and down to earth. Oh, and should you want to emulate her distinctive look, her hair dye is Blue 56.

Friends and Lovers

Finally, the 1990s saw the launch of the massively successful sitcom *Friends*. This program followed the lives of six single twenty-something New Yorkers—Ross, Chandler, Joey, Rachel, Phoebe, and Monica—as they tried to find their way in the world. When the show first began, the only mother on the program was Ross's ex-wife Susan, who had left him for another woman.

It wasn't until the later years of the *Friends* run that the friends began to have motherhood experiences of their own. Phoebe was a surrogate mother for her brother and his wife, giving birth to triplets. Phoebe wanted "to keep one," but she gave the kids over to her brother, content to merely be their cool aunt. As the series closed, Chandler and Monica had come to terms with Chandler's infertility and adopted twins. Perhaps the most significant motherhood experience on *Friends* belonged to Ross and Rachel. After a night of drunken passion, the on-again, off-again couple finds out that Rachel is pregnant. They decide that they are going to keep the baby and raise it together, but not get married.

❀

Reality Bites

The new millennium has seen the rise in popularity of reality television, so it's not surprising that a reality television show centered around a family would become a hit. What was surprising was the family featured. One could say that Roseanne Connor and Peg Bundy laid the groundwork for the widespread acceptance of Sharon Osbourne, matriarch of *The Osbournes*. The wife of noted rocker and bat-biter Ozzy Osbourne, Sharon keeps her children Jack and Kelly, along with their doddering father, in line on the wildly popular reality program.

But even in the dysfunctional environment portrayed on the show, the love shared between Sharon, her husband, and their children is readily apparent. Although the television mom has changed drastically from the days of June Cleaver, the one thing that has remained constant is the bond between television children and their mom.

Movie Mom

Most Popular Mom Movies

1. *Stepmom* (1998)
2. *Throw Momma from the Train* (1987)
3. *Terms of Endearment* (1983)
4. *Mr Mom* (1983)
5. *Baby Boom* (1987)
Source: Blockbuster Inc.

The Worst Mom: Joan Crawford

As played by Faye Dunaway in Mommie Dearest, *1981*

Perhaps the most monstrous portrayal of motherhood on screen, Faye Dunaway dons a dark wig, arched eyebrows, and stern, down-turned mouth to capture the mood of her character. Indeed, she certainly looked like the legendary silver screen actress. Based on the vengeful memoir of one of Crawford's two adopted children, Christina and Christopher, the film is delightfully awful and over the top. Christina alleges that as Crawford's movie career faltered she began to dole out emotional abuse indiscriminately and on a scale many would think impossible. One such memorable piece of advice/abuse was given to Christina about clothes storage: "No wire hangers. EVER!"

Take Five: Five Worst Mom Movies
1. The Good Mother (1988)
Directed by Leonard Nimoy
Starring: Diane Keaton and Liam Neeson

First things first—Diane Keaton ain't a good mother in this 1988 drama. Keaton plays Anna, a recently divorced mother who takes up with Leo, played by Liam Neeson, an artist with whom she begins a sordid affair. Not long after this romance begins, the villainous "bad father" arrives, seeking to take custody of their young daughter.

The reason for his return and desire to take the kid? Apparently Anna and Leo have occasionally made love while the daughter shared the same bed with them. The movie degenerates into a poorly acted series of courtroom scenes where the evil father-figure tries to wrest his daughter from her not-so-good mother.

2. Stop! Or My Mom Will Shoot (1992)
Directed by: Robert Spottiswoode
Starring: Sylvester Stallone and Estelle Getty

What studio executive gave this movie the green light? This movie starts out with Sylvester Stallone playing a tough big city cop. What's the only thing that can unnerve a steely-nerved detective like Sly? That's right, a visit from momma, played by *Golden Girls* matriarch Estelle Getty. Getty soon derails Stallone's life. She gets in the middle of gunfights and wrecks her son's gun with soap. But her nagging does help at least one person: when Stallone tries to talk a would-be suicide off a building ledge, Getty grabs a bullhorn. The berating she gives her son makes the prospective leaper realize that his life really isn't so bad—since at least he's not her son! Said noted movie critic Roger Ebert about this dud, "There isn't a laugh in this movie. Not a single one, and believe me, I was looking." On the bright side, it's only eighty-seven minutes long!

3. My Stepmother is an Alien (1988)

Directed by: Richard Benjamin
Starring: Dan Ackroyd, Kim Bassinger, and Alyson Hannigan

In this 1988 comedy, Dan Ackroyd plays a single parent and brilliant physicist who manages to harness the power of lightning to send a transmission to a distant planet. The planet responds by sending a spaceship to Earth. On board is an alien, who when in human form is the beautiful blond Kim Bassinger. The Alien comes to earth to convince Ackroyd to repeat his experiment in order to save her planet.

On Earth she does such wacky things as eat cigarette butts, drink battery acid, and dip her bare hand into boiling water—all witnessed by Ackroyd's teen daughter, played by a young Alyson Hannigan.

Ultimately this is a romantic comedy and not a science fiction affair, so illogical story holes don't really matter. Despite the fact that Bassinger would have had horrendous "ashtray breath," she uses her alien wiles to win the portly scientist's heart, as well as that of his daughter. Needless to say, this one preceded Bassinger's Oscar turn in *L.A. Confidential* by a few years.

4. Serial Mom (1994)

Directed by: John Waters
Starring: Kathleen Turner, Sam Waterston, and Ricki Lake

In this flick, Kathleen Turner plays a seemingly perfect Baltimore housewife who is the model of wifely decorum. But her normality is an illusion—Turner is actually a deranged serial killer. Her victims include a neighbor remiss at recycling and the teacher Turner mows down in her car after he dared give her child a poor grade. Trash TV talk show host Ricki Lake plays Turner's boy-crazy daughter, who enterprisingly sells t-shirts outside her mom's murder trial. While some might think that standing up for her child by running down her teacher makes Turner a good mother, we happen to think it just might teach the kid the wrong lesson.

5. The Next Best Thing (2000)

Directed by: John Schlesinger
Starring: Madonna, Rupert Everett, Benjamin Bratt

In this stinker, Los Angeles yoga instructor Abbie (Madonna) and her gay best friend Robert (Rupert Everett) attend the funeral of a gay friend felled by AIDS. Following the funeral, Abbie and Robert drown their grief in an incredible amount of liquor. When the two awaken with pounding headaches, they realize that in their drunken haze they had made love. This potentially friendship-shattering event is no big deal…until Abbie realizes that she is pregnant with Robert's baby. Of course, Abbie and Robert decide to keep the baby and raise it together.

While both Abbie and Robert insist that they are fine with the other one continuing to date, of course it turns out that this isn't really the case. When Abbie meets handsome Ben (Benjamin Bratt), Robert is consumed by jealously. Ben wants to marry Abbie and move to New York, removing Robert from his child's life. At this point this sexual comedy morphs into a courtroom drama. At no point do you ever care about Abbie, Robert, Ben or the baby. All you really care about is how much longer you have to suffer through the flick.

Take Five: Five Acting Moms

1. Meg Ryan

The beautiful Meg Ryan is known as America's sweetheart, and she has starred in such classic romantic comedies as *When Harry Met Sally* and *Sleepless in Seattle*. She has a son named Jack Henry Quaid with her ex-husband, actor Dennis Quaid.

2. Nicole Kidman

Kidman won the best actress Oscar for her role in *The Hours*. This Australian-born actress has two adopted children, Connor and Isabella, with her ex-husband. You might have heard of him—his name is Tom Cruise.

3. Reese Witherspoon

This *Legally Blonde* star and actor husband Ryan Phillipe have one daughter, Ava, and a son, Deacon.

4. Gwyneth Paltrow

This Oscar-winning star of *Shakespeare in Love* had her first child, a girl named Apple, with British rocker Chris Martin of Coldplay.

5. Angelina Jolie

Jolie, the Best Supporting Actress Oscar-winner for her work in *Girl, Interrupted*, has an adopted son from Cambodia named Maddox.

MOVIE MOM: JUDY GARLAND

Born Frances Ethel Gumm on June 10, 1922, Judy was the third daughter of retired vaudeville performers. Encouraged by her parents, Judy performed in her parents' theatre and honed her craft through singing and dancing lessons. Ready to enter the acting profession, Frances Gumm took the name Judy because she preferred its "peppy" sound. Signed to MGM at the age of thirteen, Garland would make forty-three films during her career. She achieved superstardom following the 1938 release of *The Wizard of Oz*.

ONE WOMAN AWARD SHOW

In addition to her film career, Garland acted in television, the theatre, recorded albums, and lent her voice to radio. Throughout her career, she was nominated for Emmys, won an Academy Award, a Tony, and five Grammys. Adding to her very busy schedule, she gave birth to three children: Liza Minnelli (with Vincente Minnelli, her second husband) and Lorna and Joey Luft (with her third husband, Sid Luft).

Her balancing act was made more difficult in light of her personal problems. Garland controlled her weight and aided sleep with prescription drugs. While not everyone agrees that the actress was also an alcoholic, most feel that her substance use was symptomatic of larger emotional problems.

Garland died on June 22, 1969, way too early at the age of forty-seven. The official cause of death was an accidental overdose of sleeping pills. Garland was one of only a few people who became a legend in her own time. She balanced the duties of mother, wife, and performer before her personal demons won out. It is not surprising that she took on the duties of a family. She once said: "I can live without money, but I cannot live without love."

Koo-Koo-Ka-Choo...

In the 1968 movie *The Graduate*, Anne Bancroft plays Mrs. Robinson, a man-eating, martini-swilling, iron-willed mother whose love for her daughter turns to spite and disregard. On the soundtrack, famed bards Simon & Garfunkel offer a rather different characterization. The lyrics "Hide it in a hiding place where no one ever goes—put it in your pantry with your cupcakes" and "Jesus loves you more than you will know" don't exactly paint the same picture of Mrs. Robinson as the film script. It is quite doubtful that Anne Bancroft's character baked cupcakes or was terribly concerned with whether or not Jesus loved her.

Take Five: Five Movies about the Mother-Child Bond

1. Sophie's Choice (1982)
Directed by: Alan J. Pakula
Starring: Meryl Streep and Kevin Kline

Meryl Streep is Sophie Zawistowska, a young concentration camp survivor struggling to make a new life for herself in America. She moves to New York City following the war, and takes up with Nathan (Kevin Kline), a charismatic but occasionally violent man. The film follows Sophie and Nathan's stormy relationship, and shows the evolution of Sophie's character through flashbacks of her experiences during the war. At the movie's most powerful moment, we finally learn the nature of *Sophie's Choice*—a choice no mother should have to make. Streep won an Academy Award for her stunning portrayal of Sophie.

2. Terms of Endearment (1983)

Directed by: James L. Brooks
Starring: Debra Winger, Shirley MacLaine, and Jack Nicholson

The Oscar winner for Best Picture in 1983, *Terms of Endearment* stars Shirley MacLaine as Aurora, the passionate mother of headstrong Emma, played by Debra Winger. Jack Nicholson, playing a retired astronaut, is cast as Aurora's love interest. Against her mother's advice, young Emma marries a literature professor and moves out of state. Emma's strained relationship with her mom is replicated in the relationship she has with her oldest son. Tragedy brings the family back together when Emma is hospitalized in what is ultimately a losing battle with cancer. *Terms of Endearment* won Shirley MacLaine the Academy Award for Best Actress, and Jack Nicholson the award for Best Supporting Actor.

3. Lorenzo's Oil (1992)

Directed by: George Miller
Starring: Nick Nolte and Susan Sarandon

Lorenzo's Oil is based on the true story of parents Augusto (Nick Nolte) and Michaela Odone (Susan Sarandon) as they fight to save the life of their young son Lorenzo, who in 1984 is diagnosed with adrenoleukodystrophy (ADT), a degenerative, incurable, and fatal brain disorder. Told by doctors that their son has less than twenty-four months to live, the Odone's set out to find a cure for ADT. While Augusto combs through medical journals and talks to medical experts, Michaela stays home to read and talk to Lorenzo, as she is certain that beneath his comatose exterior there lives a vibrant and alert mind.

In the end their quest is successful, and they develop what has become known as Lorenzo's oil, a substance that defeats ADT by maintaining the protective casing that surrounds nerves in the brain. As for the real life Lorenzo, although he does not have most of his physical functions, his mind is still active. Thanks to the dedication of his parents, in May of 2004 he celebrated his twenty-sixth birthday, far exceeding the bleak two-year prognosis given him by doctors twenty years earlier.

4. Mask (1985)

Directed by: Peter Bogdanovich
Starring: Cher and Eric Stoltz

This 1985 film stars Eric Stoltz as Rocky, a young adolescent with severe facial deformities caused by craniodyaphyseal dysplasia, a disease which causes calcium to accumulate in the skull, thereby making the head grow to twice its normal size. Rocky doesn't give in to his disease though, and the friendly, outgoing kid strives to have a normal life.

Cher plays Rocky's loving and protective mom Rusty, a biker chick battling a mild drug habit who does everything she can to secure Rocky's happiness, including marching into his school to demand equal rights for her son. In the end, Rocky meets a beautiful blind girl at a camp and helps his mom kick her drug habit. This movie is all the more poignant given that it is based on the true-life story of Rocky Denis.

5. One True Thing (1998)

Directed by: Carl Franklin
Starring: Renee Zellweger, Meryl Streep, and William Hurt

Renee Zellweger plays Ellen Gulden, a young career woman who quits her job, leaves her boyfriend, and returns home to help her mother Kate (Meryl Streep) battle cancer. Ellen's father George (William Hurt), a successful English professor, seems more concerned with having Ellen help keep his life in order than in having her comfort her ailing mom.

The return home changes Ellen's view of her father. Where

he once was a literary giant in her eyes, she soon begins to see him as a failed writer, trying to affect one last chance at literary immortality. We gradually see the hurt that Kate has born throughout the years over the fact that Ellen always seemed to love her father more. This, of course, isn't the case. As Kate's condition worsens, and as she comes closer and closer to expiring, her love for her husband and child manages to hold the family together. *The One True Thing* is a mother's love.

9

Moms of the Animal World

"One cannot fix one's eyes on the commonest natural production without finding food for a rambling fancy." —Jane Austen

Animals in the wild kingdom have mothers, too. How do the moms of the animal kingdom compare to those of the human world? Motherhood in the animal world can be every bit as fascinating and wondrous as our own.

Gorilla Moms

Gorillas are the largest of all primates and have always fascinated us. Perhaps it is because they are our cousins, and they represent a look back at motherhood before we had consciousness, before we were human.

Gorillas can grow up to six feet and can weigh up to five hundred pounds. For all their strength, though, they are peaceful, family-oriented, plant-eating animals.

Gorillas live in communities or "troops" of anywhere from five to thirty in any one grouping. The group is always led by a dominant male, whose job is to protect the troop as well as find food. He is known as a silverback because of the patch of silver colored fur on his back.

Female gorillas are ready to have babies when she is about eight years old and the gestation period can last from 8.3 to nine months. The scary thing for a potential new mother is now she must leave the safety of her own troop and find another troop or a lone silverback to live with.

Newborns learn to walk by six months. By eighteen months they can follow their mother on foot for short distances. Like chimps, the safest place for the young gorilla is its mother's back, as she travels through the dense vegetation of their forest home.

Young gorillas imitate what others in the troop are doing, and in doing so learn the way of the jungle. Even silverbacks play gentle with the young as they try out new skills. A young gorilla stays with its mother until it is four to six years old.

Did You Know...?

The male deep sea anglerfish mates with a female after he bites her—but he never lets go. The male's mouth gradually grows into the skin of the female, and his body merges into hers. Nearly all of the male's internal organs disappear, apart from the testes. The male spends the remainder of his life as a shrunken parasite on his mate, there only to provide the sperm that fertilizes her eggs at breeding time.

Newborn Critters ❀

- A baby harp seal doubles its weight in only five days after birth, thanks to the amount of protein in its mother's milk. It takes a horse sixty days to double its birth weight.

- A baby baleen whale depends on its mother's milk diet for at least six months.

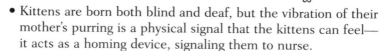

- Kittens are born both blind and deaf, but the vibration of their mother's purring is a physical signal that the kittens can feel—it acts as a homing device, signaling them to nurse.

- When baby opossums are born, they are so small that an entire litter can fit in a tablespoon. They live inside their mother's pouch for three months before climbing out and riding on her back.

African Elephants ✿

Like humans, elephants do not have any specific mating season. The reproductive rate is higher during the rainy season compared to that of droughts, but that is the extent of the deviation. One area where they do trump their human counterparts is that their gestation period lasts some 20–22 months. When the calves are finally born, they weigh in at more than two hundred fifty pounds (slightly heavier than your seven-pound human).

The calf can see, smell, and almost walk a relatively short time after birth. The calf follows its mother as soon as it can walk. One of the more fascinating aspects of motherhood among African elephants is that a calf is guarded and taken care of by all mothers, young females who assist the calf's mother, almost like babysitters. While the biological mothers are sleeping, the babysitters protect the babies and retrieve them if they stray too far. Related elephant cows in the herd also frequently suckle each other's calves.

Mothers give birth every four to nine years and the older calves are weaned a few months before the next is born.

Elephant society is based on a matriarchal system. The matriarch is typically the oldest female and it is she who leads a clan of six to twelve elephants throughout her lifetime. Only closely related females and their offspring are part of this herd (males wander alone or in bachelor herds once they reach maturity). The herd's well-being depends on the guidance of the matriarch.

She determines when they eat, rest, bathe or drink. The closeness of the herd allows the rest of the elephants to acquire knowledge to be used when needed.

As the matriarch begins to be limited by advancing age, around 50–60 years old, the next oldest replaces her and she is either abandoned or leaves by herself.

Motherly Instinct in the Animal World

St. Augustine once asked: "What tigress is there that does not purr over her young ones, and fawn upon them in tenderness?" This saintly churchman was on to something. Human moms are not the only ones to love, protect, and sacrifice for their kids.

Take Five: Five Animals That Eat Their Young (And Moms of Teenagers Know Why)

- Gerbil
- Lion
- Praying mantis
- Crow
- Asian forest scorpion

Trumpeter Swan

Trumpeter swans are unusual in the wild, not only for their beauty, but also because they form monogamous pairings that last a lifetime. Trumpeter swans are usually the first waterfowl to appear on breeding grounds in the northern U.S., arriving as the ice barely melts in the spring.

They begin courtship behavior at this point, which includes bobbing their heads and quivering their wings while facing each other. Breeding usually happens between their fourth to sixth year. (Breeding in captivity may take years before a pair is suitably comfortable to produce fertile eggs.)

The incubation period for eggs usually lasts thirty-three to thirty-seven days. When the mother swan leaves the nest to feed or bathe, she covers the eggs with nest material. The male is a partner in this as well. He guards the nest, defending it against any danger.

Cygnets hatch in June and weigh in at seven ounces. They take to the water after only a day or two and feed in shallow water areas. Cygnets stay with their parents through the summer and migrate with them to wintering grounds in October or November. They will also return with their parents back to summer grounds in the spring. They remain in sibling groups until they are about two years old. Swans may live up to thirty-five years in the wild.

Mother Crocodile

Ferocious though they may be, mother crocodiles (called cows) are caring critters when it comes to their babes. Crocodiles are one of the few reptiles to protect their young. An expectant mom settles in by her nest, patiently waiting for the eggs to hatch. She even offers a hand—or a tooth—to help her babies break free. After the babies hatch, mom carries them to the water, and protects them until they are almost a year old— she might even give them a ride on her back. Should any predator come too close, the mother crocodile will threaten or attack. Some species will even call her babies to swim into the mouth for protection—fooling predators into thinking she has swallowed them.

Dolphins

Dolphins can be found in all oceans of the world and the gregarious nature of some species has made them a curiosity to humans since time began. Male bottlenose dolphins become sexually mature between five and thirteen years of age, with females becoming sexually mature between nine and fourteen years.

There is no actual mating season for dolphins, but almost all of their mating activity is foreplay. Much of that activity is chasing each other around and raking each other with their teeth.

According to the Dolphin Research Center, mothers double their intake of food following the birth of their babies. Intervals between calves vary from about three to five years.

The babies are born tail first, weigh anywhere from twenty-five to forty lbs., and are generally three to four feet long. The baby dolphin swims in a position next to its mother called the echelon position, helping it to catch mom's slipstream, in effect, allowing the baby to not work as hard in order to keep up with its mother.

Females with calves often congregate in pods and other females have been seen assisting with a birth. They've also been seen to serve as babysitters. Like humans, the best way for a female dolphin to learn how to care for a calf is to be around a baby. Female dolphins seem to have a unique mothering style.

Adult male dolphins are absentee fathers and play no role in raising their young. They go off on their own, coming together in groups of two or three, sometimes forming what scientist's call "pair bond." Pair bonded males will stay together for an extended period, if not all of their lives.

Before His Time

In 340 BC, Aristotle observed that dolphins gave birth to live young that were attached to their mothers by umbilical cords. For this reason, he considered dolphins and related creatures to be mammals. Twenty-four centuries later, biologists agreed with him.

A Day's Work

All Nature seems at work. Slugs leave their lair—
The bees are stirring, birds are on a wing—
And Winter is slumbering in the open air.
—Samuel Taylor Coleridge

Chimpanzees

Chimpanzees grow anywhere from three feet to four feet tall. Chimps live in communities made up of family members and other family groups. Individual family groups number six to ten, but a community can easily have as many as a hundred members. They are the most social of all the apes.

Usually communities are led by an adult male chimp, but sometimes leadership is spread among several males. Male chimps almost always stay in the community into which they were born, but females transfer to other communities when they become adults. Chimps use a variety of methods to communicate, including body language, facial expressions, hand-clapping, grooming, and kissing to communicate within their community.

Grooming is one of the single most important social activities engaged in by chimps. It is through grooming that chimps nourish friendships, comfort each other, and patch up disagreements. Grooming shows us just how socially sophisticated and similar they are to their human cousins. In some instances, mothers of newborns are groomed in hopes of getting a closer look at the newcomer.

Female chimps give birth for the first time when they are between twelve and fifteen years old. Newborns learn quickly to cling to their mother's belly, later learning to transfer to get around by piggy-back.

Young chimps are breastfed until they are three years old, and are usually walking on their own at four. Chimps will usually stay with their mother until age seven, learning the skills needed to survive. The bond between mother and chimp is so strong that it will last a lifetime.

Sockeye Mom

Sockeye salmon moms pay the ultimate price for motherhood: their lives. When it's time to spawn, the expectant mother salmon uses a navigational sense of direction that scientists do not fully understand (but which might be connected to the earth's magnetic fields) to travel long distances—often thousands of miles—to return from the ocean to the river or stream of her own birth.

On her journey, the mother salmon undergoes a metamorphosis—her head shape and color change rapidly. Once at her spawning destination, the mother digs a nest with her tail and deposits two thousand to forty-five hundred eggs. Spent by her journey, the mother salmon dies within weeks of spawning and her decomposing body becomes part of the food chain that will nourish her babies.

Blue Whale Mom

Blue whales breed almost exclusively in the winter to early spring. Warm waters near the surface provide the backdrop to the mating dance. The gestation period of 11–12 months culminates when the calf is born tail first near the surface in warm, shallow waters. The newborn instinctively swims to the surface and within ten seconds is gulping for its first breath. The mother helps the newborn to the surface by using her flippers; within 30 minutes the baby whale is swimming.

The newborn calf is typically twenty-five feet long and weighs in at six to eight tons. Calves drink 50–200 pounds of milk each day. In its first several weeks of life, it gains ten pounds an hour, or a little over two hundred pounds a day.

The mother and her calf may stay together for a year or longer, until the calf is about forty-five feet long. Young whales don't reach maturity, however, until aged five to ten years. Blue whales go on to live individually or in very small groups and frequently swim in pairs. Unlike much of the animal kingdom, females are larger than males. The largest of the blue whales weighed in at one hundred fifty tons and had a heart that weighed about one thousand pounds circulating some14,000 pounds of blood.

North American Killdeer Mom

This mom is no birdbrain. If her nest of babies is threatened, she will lure predators away from it by pretending she has a broken wing. Sometimes this tactic works—other times the mom loses her life to save her babies.

Platypus Mom

The mother platypus is a mammal that lays eggs like birds or reptiles. It usually lays two or three eggs, and keeps them warm by placing them on her belly and covering them with her tail. The baby platypus feeds on its mother's milk, which comes out of glands—not teats—on the mother's skin. The babies lick the milk off the mother's fur.

❀

Kangaroo Moms

If you've always thought of the kangaroo as one of a kind, you might be surprised to know that it belongs to a much larger family, one with as many as fifty-six species. It is only the larger species that are called kangaroos and wallaroos.

Big-footed marsupials, the kangaroo evolved in Australia. Males of the species are known as boomers, females as flyers, and the young as joeys. The female has her famous pouch in front of her body in which she carries the young after birth.

The largest kangaroos stand over six feet and weigh almost one hundred fifty pounds and can reach a running speed of 35 mph, with leaps as long as twenty-four feet. Kangaroos live alone or in small groups, but come together in larger groups when food is scarce.

Kangaroos have short pregnancies. A red kangaroo joey is tiny when it is born—just one inch long! After it is born, the tiny baby crawls up the fur on the mother's belly and into her pouch. It immediately attaches itself to the teat and suckles for a long time. The mother cleans the inside of the pouch with her lips and often holds it open with her hands.

After three months, the joey begins to go out and look for food, returning to the pouch between expeditions. The baby's stay in the pouch may last five to nine months. Young reds become independent from their mother at an early age, and in their harsh environment, young roos must learn quickly how to survive if they are to avoid predators such as dingos and eagles.

❀

A female kangaroo is almost always pregnant. Often, she will have three offspring to keep on track—an embryo in the womb, a joey in her pouch, and a youngster at her heels.

Giant Panda Moms

Panda's have wowed children and adults for a thousand years. Such is the fascination with the panda in the U.S. that the Washington's National Zoo pays the Chinese Wildlife Conservation Association $1.5 million annually to rent two pandas from the Chinese government for ten years.

Add to the fact that the zoo spent a further $2.7 million on renovations for the pandas' residence, which includes air-conditioned caves and sand wallows and several "microclimates" with varying temperature and humidity, and you get a sense of what stars pandas really are.

Giant pandas reach breeding maturity between four and eight years of age. Female pandas ovulate only once a year, and only for two to three days. The slow breeding rate is one of the reasons there are fewer than a thousand pandas in the wild.

Female giant pandas give birth between ninety-five and one hundred sixty days after mating. Although females may give birth to two young, usually only one survives. Newborns are completely helpless and weigh as little as three ounces. Except for members of the kangaroo family, a giant panda baby is the smallest mammal newborn relative to its mother's size.

The mother nurses her cub for eight to nine months, but the cub is not nutritionally weaned until the end of the first year. For safety and to learn the ways of the world, cubs can stay with their mothers for up to three years before going it alone.

Octopus Mom

Most moms wish they had eight arms…and this real octa-armed creature is sure a devoted mom. When a mother octopus is ready to lay her eggs—all sixty-thousand of them—she settles herself in a den. When she lays the eggs, she hangs them from the roof of the den, and guards them with her life—literally. While they incubate, a span of from one to about five months, the mom never leaves their side. She won't even go in search of a bite to eat, fasting instead. After all of the babies hatch, the mother dies of starvation. This is an amazing sacrifice, especially when one considers that on average, just two of her babies will survive to adulthood.

Penguin Moms

Breeding seasons for penguins vary from species to species. The king penguin has the longest breeding season of all the penguin species, lasting some fourteen to sixteen months and a female king penguin may produce a chick twice in every three breeding seasons. She may produce two chicks during breeding seasons.

Courtship varies from species to species, but each has elaborate visual and auditory displays. In many species, males are often the first to establish a nest, with the intention of building a home and attracting a mate. Unlike most of the animal kingdom, penguin species are largely monogamous, at least during a mating season. Mate selection is up to the female, and it is the females that compete for the males. Once a female has paired, she usually selects the same male each season.

Both male and female penguins spell each off during the incubation period. As if to drop a hint, the female emperor penguin simply pushes the egg to the top of her partner's feet. The male fasts throughout the courtship, nesting, and incubation periods, living off reserves of body fat. Male emperor penguins go even further. If the chick happens to hatch before the female returns, in one of the remarkable feats of nature, the male, despite fasting, produces a substance from his esophagus to feed the chick.

Both parents feed the chick regurgitated food. Depending on the species, the first weeks to a year are crucial to the survival of the chick. It is during this period that the chick grows water-proof feathers and is able to enter water, becoming independent.

Polar Bear Mom

Female polar bears reach sexual maturity at about four years of age, two years ahead of their male counterparts. They don't successfully mate however, until eight to ten years and older.

Breeding season is in April and May when polar bears find themselves in the best seal-hunting holes. Male polar bears are diligent in their pursuit of females, and have followed the tracks of breeding females for the length of sixty miles.

Females breed once every three years, and as a result there are about three adult males to every female. Competing males fight brutally until the strongest or largest male is the victor.

Gestation lasts about eight months, and female polar bears need to gain at least four hundred pounds for a successful preg-nancy. Females search for dens in late October to protect new-born cubs (normally born between November and January). They will not come out of their den again until the weather begins to relent in late March or early April.

During their first few weeks of life, polar bear cubs stay close to their mothers just to keep warm and nurse almost all of the time. At birth, newborns are hairless and weigh in at just over a pound.

Mothers are so protective of their young, they will risk their own lives in their cubs' defense. Polar bears, though, are mostly solitary, often only coming together to breed.

143

Did You Know…?

Milk from polar bear mothers is about 35 percent fat, making it one of the fattiest of mothers' milk.

Mother Nature Quote

"Nature and books belong to the eyes that see them."
—Ralph Waldo Emerson

American Alligator Mom

The sexual maturity of American alligators is determined by length, about six feet, and than age. (They grow to about eight feet.) Usually though, maturity sets in around ten to twelve years old. American alligators have been known to reach up to fifty years old in the wild.

Courtship lasts a month, with the male roaring to attract females, and just importantly, to scare off other males. After the mating is complete, the female builds a nest. It is here that only two months later she will lay some thirty-five to fifty eggs, covering them for a sixty-five-day incubation period.

In another mystery of nature, the sex of the offspring is determined by the temperature of the nest. In temperatures above 93° F the offspring are male; below 86°F, offspring will be female; in temperatures in between 86° and 93°, the nest will have both sexes.

Following the incubation period, the young hatchlings beckon by making high-pitched noises from inside the egg, letting their mothers know that it is time to remove the nesting material. When they hatch, they will measure about six to eight inches. The mother helps her new hatchlings out of the nest, and carrying them in her mouth to the water.

It is here her new hatchlings live in small groups called "pods." It is not an easy life, though, with upwards of 80 percent of young alligators falling prey to birds and other animals.

Mothers do everything they can, defending their young during these first few years. Uncommon among reptiles, mothers provide a long period of maternal care to their young. Even after young alligators leave, they may stay return to stay with her for a few days to a year.

Who Do You Call Mom?

Sea horses are unique in the world, in that the male, not the female becomes "pregnant." The female releases her eggs into a pouch on the male's abdomen. He fertilizes them and they grow there.

10

Thanks, Mom

"A man loves his sweetheart the most, his wife the best, but his mother the longest." —Irish Proverb

Mothers often feel theirs is a thankless job, but adulthood brings new appreciation of a mom's love and sacrifice.

Americans Love Their Mom

- According to a Harris Interactive poll, 9 percent of Americans say that mom is their hero.

- According to Gallup, 53 percent of Americans say that mom is the person who had the greatest influence on their growing up years and 48 percent of moms say that their own mothers are their best friends.

- Seventy-six percent of Americans say that their relationship with mom is "very positive," while only 3 percent describe their relationship with mom as negative.

- Even teens, that most self-absorbed species of human, appreciate mom. Seventy-one percent of American teens say they have an excellent or very good relationship with mom, and that they are three times more likely to rely solely on mom than on dad when they have important decisions to make.

That's Cool

A mother from Delaware sent two hundred air conditioning units to American troops sweltering in Iraq. Frankie Mayo, a housewife from the town of Bear, had a twenty-one-year old son serving there with the U.S. military. She said she wanted to do something for him after he emailed her saying he was fine, except for the 145° F temperature in his army-issue tent. Mayo's motherly concern has blossomed into a full-scale campaign to bring relief to American soldiers in the service of their country. "Operation Air Conditioner" has already delivered fourteen air conditioners to her son's base. As the units arrived, some of the soldiers fell to their knees to hug the relief-giving appliances.

Heavyweight

The heaviest newborn baby to survive delivery was born to Signora Carmelina Fedele of Aversa, Italy, in September 1955.

- The healthy "little" bundle of joy weighed in at 22 lb, 8 oz. This world record was tied on May 24, 1982, when a second hefty baby boy was born in South Africa.

- By way of contrast, the tiniest baby to survive weighed in at a mere 10 oz.

Quotes Honoring Mom

"There never was a woman like her. She was gentle as a dove and brave as a lioness... The memory of my mother and her teachings were, after all, the only capital I had to start life with, and on that capital I have made my way."
—Andrew Jackson, U.S. president

"Life began with waking up and loving my mother's face."
—George Elliot

"Men are what their mothers made them."
—Ralph Waldo Emerson

"When I stopped seeing my mother with the eyes of a child, I saw the woman who helped me give birth to myself."
—Nancy Friday, on the transition to independence

"Mother: the most beautiful word on the lips of mankind."
—Kahil Gibran

"Mother is the name for God on the lips and hearts of little children."
—William Makepeace Thackery

"Whatever else is unsure in this stinking dunghill of a world, a mother's love is not."
—James Joyce

"The greatest difference which I find between my mother and the rest of the people whom I have known is this, and it is a remarkable one: while others felt a strong interest in a few things, she felt a strong interest in the whole world and everything and everybody in it."
—Mark Twain

"My mother made a brilliant impression upon my childhood life. She shone for me like the evening star—I loved her dearly."
—Winston Churchill

"My mother was the most beautiful woman I ever saw...All I am I owe to my mother...I attribute all my success in life to the moral, intellectual, and physical education I received from her."
—George Washington

MOTHER THERESA:
MOTHER TO THE WORLD'S POOR

No woman evokes the idea of a mother willing to sacrifice her life for her "children" more than does Mother Theresa. She was born Agnes Bonxha Bojaxhiu in Macedonia on August 27, 1910. At the age of twelve, she received what she described as her call from God. At eighteen, she left her home and joined the Sisters of Loreto, an Irish community of nuns who had missions in India.

After a few months of training in Dublin, she was sent to India where, on May 24, 1931, she took her initial vows as a nun. From 1931 to 1948, Mother Theresa taught high school in Calcutta, all the while disturbed by the poverty and suffering she saw outside her convent walls. In 1948, she was granted permission to leave her convent school and devote herself to working among the poor living in Calcutta's slums. Although she had no funds, she started an open-air school for children of the Calcutta ghettos.

In October 1950, Mother Theresa founded The Missionaries of Charity, whose primary task was to care for people no one else was prepared to look after. The compassionate care that Mother Theresa gave to the forgotten poor of India has been recognized by a number of awards and distinctions, including the Pope John Paul XXIII Peace Prize (1971) and the Nobel Peace Prize (1979).

As a nun, Mother Theresa married her faith, and could bear no children of her own. And yet, through her work, she became a loving mother-figure to thousands of impoverished and down-trodden "children" the world over. Mother Theresa died on September 5, 1997, but her name and deeds live on.

Subconscious Mom

Research shows that both men and women choose marriage partners based on perceptions of their mothers. Those who see mothers as stern are more likely to select a strict mate. Those who think of mom as gentle are likely to fall for a tender mate.

Take Five: Top Five Nations That Thank Mom

Each year, nations are ranked according to how well they meet the needs of mothers. America placed a disappointing eleventh in the 2003 Mother's Index. In rank order, the top five nations are:

1. Sweden
2. Denmark
3. Norway
4. Switzerland
5. Finland

Source: Mother's Index

Quotable Mom

"Never say anything on the phone that you wouldn't want your mother to hear at your trial." —Sydney Biddle Barrows, *notorious American socialite and brothel-owner*

Oedipus Rex, Or, You Are So Beautiful to Me

- According to a survey by Clairol, 80 percent of women think mom is beautiful.

- Seventy-two percent of men think this.

- Teenaged daughters also think mom is quite grand. Eighty-three percent say that their mom is beautiful.

Take Five: Top Five Pieces of Mom's Advice That Have Benefited Your Career

1. "Always remember to say please and thank-you."
2. "Just because everyone else jumps off a bridge, it doesn't mean you should too."
3. "Say your prayers every night."
4. "Look both ways before crossing the street."
5. "Share with others."

(Surprisingly, always wear clean underwear was not on the list.)

Source: Monster.com

Chefs Extraordinaire

- Seventy-one percent of us say that we learned to cook from our moms.

- Only 12 percent thank dad for our culinary skills, according to Tasting Arizona.

- Two-thirds of employees say that their mom would do a better job at resolving employee disputes, according to a survey by Management Recruitment International.

- Sixty-two percent say that mom would handle their company's finances better, and 80 percent say that their mom's ethics are the same or stronger than their company's CEO.

If I Had a Million Dollars

- In a Hallmark survey of kids aged six to ten, 29 percent of American kids explained that if they had "all the money in the world" they would pay mom $1,000,000 for all she does.

- Incredibly, 78 percent of kids thought that their own mom was worth more than pop idol Britney Spears. High praise indeed.

It Takes Mom to Know Mom

- Most moms—fully 84 percent—feel that they came to know their own moms better as they too became mothers, according to babycenter.com.

- Moms value the expertise of their own moms: 66 percent consult their mom about their parenting styles.

- Sixty-four percent of moms say that their own mom had happy kids.

- Sixty-eight percent say that mom is a good influence on their own children.

- Eighty percent of grandmothers feel their daughter spends the right amount of time with their grandchildren.

> ### Quotable Mom
> *"Only a mother knows a mother's fondness."*
> —Lany Mary Wortley Montagu ❧

Quotable Mom

"What do girls do who haven't any mothers to help them through their troubles?" —Louisa May Alcott

Things Mom Will Do for Her Kids

Monkee Mike Nesmith's mother, Bette Nesmith Graham was the inventor of Liquid Paper correction fluid. She sold the rights to the Gillette Corporation in 1979 for $47.5 million and when she died in 1980, she left half of her fortune to her son Michael.

Thank You Very Much

Elvis Presley's mom, Gladys, loved her boy. The king slept in the same bed with his mother, until he reached puberty. Until Elvis entered high school, his mom walked him back and forth to school every day and made him take along his own silverware so that he wouldn't catch germs from the other kids.

Gladys forbade young Elvis from going swimming or doing anything that might endanger him. The two of them also conversed in a strange baby talk that only they could understand. For all her attention and devotion, Elvis presumably told his mom, "Thank you, thank you very much."

Quotable Mom

"God sees us through our Mothers' eyes and rewards us for our virtues."
—Ganeshan Venkatarman, Indian philosopher

SHARON OSBOURNE

If ever there was a family that needed a strong mother figure, it is that of rocker Ozzy Osbourne and his stalwart wife, Sharon. In 1970, Sharon Arden met her future husband, the rebellious and controversial lead singer of Black Sabbath, a rock band managed by her father. But it was not love at first sight. Sharon and Ozzy knew each other for nine years before they finally started to date.

Sharon assumed Ozzy's management and was instrumental in negotiating a deal for his solo career. In 1982, Sharon and Ozzy were married on a beach in Honolulu. In the 1980s, the Osbournes had three children. Their first daughter Aimee was born in 1983, a second daughter, Kelly, born in 1984, and in 1985, the family was completed with the arrival of son, Jack. All the while that Sharon was brilliantly managing Ozzie's up and down career, she raised the couple's three children, as well as two stepchildren.

OZ

Sharon also organized Ozzfest—an annual festival that debuted in 1996, and that today grosses $20 million a year. In 2002, Sharon stepped out from backstage. This matriarch and her family have become phenomenally famous in the outrageous roles they play on MTV—themselves.

As she has battled cancer, counselled her oft-confused husband, and comforted her rebellious teenagers, Sharon's maternal strength and wisdom has shone through. Her decision to end the real-life show because of its effects on her kids won Sharon's mothering further accolades.

A Mother's Love

A female's tendency to "care" begins early. In a study of behaviours exhibited by two year old, girls showed more sympathy for a crying baby than did boys. Boys would hold back; girls would pat the babies on the head, according to a study by the National Institute of Mental Health.

Moms Know They Are Loved

Eighty-five percent of American moms say that their families appreciate them enough, according to the Gallup Organization.

JACQUELINE KENNEDY: FIRST LADY, PUBLISHER, MOTHER

Jacqueline Kennedy is one of America's most beloved mothers. In a life marred by heartbreak, punctuated by tragedy and lived in a fish-bowl of media scrutiny, Jackie tried to give her children happy lives and protect from them from prying media.

Born Jacqueline Bouvier in 1929 to John Vernon Bouvier III and Janet Lee, Jackie enjoyed a privileged upbringing. After earning a degree in French literature, Jackie worked as a photographer for a Washington newspaper—the job she held when she met and fell in love with a young Massachusetts senator named John F. Kennedy (the son of Rose Kennedy, another legendary American mom).

In September 1953, the two were married, and soon began a family. The tragic stillbirth of a daughter was followed by the 1957 birth of Caroline Bouvier, a healthy baby girl. Three year's later, in 1960, John Jr. made his appearance in the world.

Later that year, John F. Kennedy announced his candidacy for President. His election in November 1960 made Jacqueline the third youngest First Lady in American history. The Kennedys were the first President and First Lady in almost a century to raise a young family in the White House.

FIRST MOM

As First Lady, Jacqueline brought culture and the arts to the White House. The First Lady was, however, adamant about the paramount importance of motherhood and explained in an interview that "if you bungle raising your children, I don't think whatever else you do well matters very much."

Jackie did her best to shield her children from the media glare surrounding their powerful father. The media respected the First Lady's wishes, and granted a modicum of privacy in August 1963 when tragedy struck the young couple. Their third son, Patrick, was born prematurely and died at just two days old. Jacqueline must still have been reeling from this loss four months later on November 22, 1963.

That day, as the motorcade of Jacqueline and President Kennedy was winding its way through the streets of Dallas, it came under fire. President John F. Kennedy was fatally wounded and died hours later. Thirty-four-year-old Jacqueline Kennedy was left a widow. America watched and grieved as Jacqueline planned a state funeral for her husband.

In 1968, Jacqueline married shipping magnate Aristotle Onassis—a union that lasted until Onassis's death in 1975. Widowed yet again, Jacqueline committed herself to a successful publishing career. Over Christmas holidays in 1993, she was diagnosed with cancer. Jacqueline Kennedy Onassis was surrounded by her children on May 19, 1994 when she succumbed to her illness. In his eulogy, John Jr. remembered his mother fondly. Citing three of her attributes, John Kennedy described his beloved mom in these terms: "love of words, the bonds of home and family, and her spirit of adventure."

11

Medical Mom

Long before there were doctors and hospitals, long before there was "germ theory" or Medicare, mothers were the medical providers for their families, creating and administering health care, and overseeing births, illnesses, and deaths. A family's health was largely left up to mom.

Women were acknowledged as having a major, if not the major role in healing and medicine. Medical schools of ancient Egypt at Heliopolis and Sais often taught females all that Egyptian medicine had to offer.

In 4th c. BC Greece, a noble woman named Philistia often gave lectures to packed audiences on homeopathy and medicine. In AD 5th c. Eudoxia, the Empress and wife of Roman Emperor Theodosius founded a hospital in Jerusalem.

When the monastic communities began to become centers of learning, including the art of medicine, many nuns took up the discipline. In the twelfth century, Hildegard von Bingen, a well-known nun and mystic, wrote two definitive medical manuscripts.

Mom Gets No Respect

Things didn't always go right for women medical practitioners. Geoffrey Chaucer, writing in the fourteenth century, satirized women's role in healing, when he wrote an account of the wife of the Chanticleer nearly poisoning her husband with her numerous remedies.

While the role of women in medicine was largely informal, their official role in hospitals and medical facilities outside the home was kept in check. The Council of Trent, meeting in the fifteenth century, even passed a resolution banning women from having official roles in hospitals.

By the sixteenth and seventeenth centuries, women were considered "empirics," simply medical practitioners who worked in the home, yet barred from studying advanced medicine in the newly found faculties of medicine in the new universities of Europe. Women's role in professional medicine was largely that of a midwife or a wet-nurse, often being present in professional medical situations only when a woman needed a physical examination.

Doctor Mom

In the eighteenth century, women were acknowledged as having a homeopathic role in medicine, but still largely confined to the household. Hundreds of household manuals, complete with home remedies and nutrition guides, were published, all with a clear focus to help mom keep the family healthy.

The role of mom as "Dr. Mom" was further challenged in the late nineteenth century as medicine was professionalized and became the domain of specially trained male doctors who scoffed at moms' practical medical knowledge. As the pharmaceutical industry gained steam, and home remedies were patented and sold commercially, Mom's expertise in home remedies was soon no longer necessary.

Today, we still look to Mom whenever something goes wrong. She may not have all the expert medical advice, but that's ok. She knows where to get it, and sometimes we just need a hug and someone to bring us another box of Kleenex. And every kid knows that only Mom can put Band-Aids on the right way.

Early American Mom: Caring for the Ill

In early America, pioneer moms had to make do with what they had, which most often was very little. Reliant on the wild environments around them, and distant from doctors and dentists, together they concocted a wide-ranging pharmacopoeia. In times of sickness it was the mother's job to relieve suffering and exact cures for their husbands and children. As a result, moms, more than any other family members, were subjected to their own bouts with illness.

Mom's Home Remedies

- Earaches were treated by dropping warm oil in the ear, and placing a bag full of hot ashes on the outer ear.

- Nosebleeds were treated by having the stricken patient sniff vinegar up their nostrils.

- Toothaches were treated by having the afflicted rinse with salt water, then placing a hot compact on the offending tooth.

- Antiseptic table salt was widely used to prevent infection.

- Sore throats were treated with the application of a bandage consisting of well-peppered bacon sewn into a woolen cloth.

- The much-dreaded croup was treated by creating a steam bath for the child out of a washtub, a kettle and a wool blanket. The child's chest would be rubbed with goose grease, and then he or she would be wrapped in a hot blanket and placed somewhere warm, free from drafts.

- Foul tasting castor oil was deemed effective preventative treatment for most illnesses, much to children's chagrin.

- Hives were treated with a soda water sponge bath and milk and honey taken internally.

- Infection or blood poison caused by stepping on a rusty nail or an inflamed blister was treated by soaking the wound in Epsom salt brine.

- For pneumonia, patients were bathed in very hot water, then tucked into bed with hot woolen blankets, given a large drink of "hot sling," made of gin and molasses, which forced perspiration.

- Tea made from watermelon seeds was said to regulate the kidneys.

- Honey and horehound were widely known as cough remedies.

- Cuts and infections were treated with various poultices made of bread and milk, crushed onion, crushed burdock leaves and sugar, or soft pine gum.

Victorian Mom: Caring for the Ill

For moms in the late nineteenth century, home remedies were all the rage. Hundreds of general household books were being produced, and most contained a wide variety of home remedies for various ailments. It was mother's job to take care of any minor ailments at home, because hospitals were reserved for the dying. Doctors would do few home visits, so mom would often just confer with doctor on a trip into town, but most often she was on her own.

As "scientific medicine" developed, and hospitals became places of medical research, more and more of the ill spent time in hospitals. From 1900 to 1920, the total number of hospital beds in America doubled, and didn't double again for another fifty years.

Suddenly, books like *Carter's Little Pills* and *Lydia Pinkham's Potions*—once very influential home remedy books—were out of vogue, and by the twentieth century, many household books had stopped listing home remedies altogether. They may have been disappearing, but they were not forgotten. Here is another sample of mom's home remedies:

- A mixture of goose grease melted together with horseradish juice, mustard, and turpentine was a common application to stop the aches and pains of rheumatism.

- If you were suffering from a headache, Mom might be instructed to give you a concoction of salt, vinegar, and whisky or brandy. One home remedy book referred to it as a "good cooling wash for headache and inflammation of the brain."

- Chapped hands? No problem. Submerge your hand into warm mutton fat taken from a sheep's udders to take care of it.

- Warts were no problem for Mom, either. The juices from a cut apple rubbed over a wart for several minutes were believed effective. The wart was promised to drop off in a few days.

- If someone was found prone to hysterics, Mom was advised to take some finely pounded caraway seeds, mix it with a small amount of ginger and salt, and to spread it on bread. Sufferers were advised to take it preferably in the morning or in the evening before going to sleep.

- One of the biggest killers in Victorian England was tuberculosis. The most effective remedy prescribed was to take a sea voyage in a warm climate, combined with pure air and nutritious food.

MARTHA BALLARD, MOTHER AND MIDWIFE

Martha Ballard is representative of so many women of the 18th century United States. Born Martha Moore in central Massachusetts in 1735, she was married at just 19 to Ephraim Ballard and together she and Ephraim raised nine children.

There is little question Martha treated her family's ailments throughout their lives, but she is best known for her role as midwife in Hallowell, Maine. In a diary kept by Martha between 1785 and 1812, she recounts her role as a respected healer and midwife. During this time she delivered no fewer than 816 babies to neighboring women, calling for a doctor just twice. Though Martha was paid for her service by the women of her small Maine community, she saw her midwifery as a calling and a gift.

By the end of the eighteenth century, midwives like Martha Ballard began to have their roles challenged by men. Male doctors began to build their medical practices by assisting in uncomplicated births—normal births that had previously been the exclusive domain of women. "Male midwives" became a controversy across the United States.

DR. ELIZABETH BLACKWELL

Not all moms practiced medicine unofficially. Elizabeth Blackwell was the first woman, and the first mom, to become a licensed medical doctor. Born in England to a wealthy family, Elizabeth Blackwell moved to the United States with her family in 1832. When her father died, leaving the family in economic ruin, her mother sought to support her family by opening a private school in Cincinnati.

It was at this school that Elizabeth's interest in medicine was piqued. She believed that women ought to have the opportunity to consult a female physician about their medical concerns. Determined to fill this gap in the medical field, she set out to find a medical school that would allow a female pupil to enroll. She was rejected by all major schools. Only the Geneva Medical College in New York state accepted her application, and then only because they believed it to be a practical joke.

When staff and students realized that Elizabeth meant business, they were horrified, but were eventually won over by her persistence. In 1849, Elizabeth became the first woman to graduate from medical school and the first woman doctor of the modern era.

RETURN TO EUROPE

She practiced her profession in Europe—in England and France—but when in 1851 she sought work in New York, she was resoundingly refused a position or even office space in which to start her own practice. And so, she began to see women and children in her home, where she built her practice.

Elizabeth Blackwell never married, but she became a mother in 1854 when she adopted an orphan girl, Katharine Barry. In 1868 Elizabeth and her sister opened the United State's first women's medical college. In 1869, Elizabeth returned to England, where she was appointed professor of gynecology at the London School of Medicine for Children, a post she held until a serious fall down a flight of stairs forced her to retire in 1907. Dr. Elizabeth Blackwell died in England in 1910.

Women in Professional Medicine

Despite the fact that women's role in medicine diminished as the field became professionalized, the role of women has steadily increased in importance.

- The first medical college for women in America, The Women's Medical College of Pennsylvania, opened in 1850.

- By the end of the nineteenth century, there were nineteen medical colleges devoted solely to the education of women.

- By the 1950s, however, only 5.5 percent of entering medical students were women.

- By the 1970s, 22.4 percent of entering medical students were women.

- Today, while the number of women who are full-time faculty members at medical schools is at 28 percent, women now account for 45.6 percent of all entering medical students.

Did You Know...?

Equal parts of liquid Benadryl and Maalox, generously smoothed on baby's tender bottom, makes a wonderful treatment for diaper rash.

Survey Says

- Ninety-nine percent of parents are happy to treat their children's ailments with over-the-counter remedies, according to a survey conducted by the Consumer Health Information Center and Developing Patient Partnerships.

- Thirty-nine percent of parents are concerned that their children will pick up bugs at school.

Excellent

- Eighty-two percent of children in America are considered to be in excellent or very good health, according to a recent national survey.

- According to the Children's National Medical Center, 85 percent of pediatricians say that the state of children's health care in the U.S. today is excellent.

- A quarter of all school children have never missed even a day of school due to illness.

- There's still work to be done, however: 88 percent said that too many children do not have access to quality health care for a variety of reasons, including insurance coverage, and transportation to doctor's offices.

We Hear Your Pain

- Ear infections are one of the most common childhood ailments, second only to the common cold.

- By the time they are three years old, more than 85 percent of kids will have had an ear infection, and 35 percent will have had three such painful ailments.

Did You Know...?

- The common cold costs Americans $40 billion a year. And no wonder—there are more than two hundred different viruses that can cause the common cold. Americans get a lot of them—about five hundred million each year—and kids lose lots of school thanks to the nasty bug.

- How much time? More than 189 million school days each year to be exact. Add that to the fact that parents lose 126 million workdays to stay home with their children and you are talking serious time. On average, American children have 6–8 colds a year.

Placebo Effect

A new study conducted at Penn State Children's Hospital has shown that over the counter cold remedies are no more effective than placebos.

Mom's Little Helper: Band-Aids

Back in 1920, newlyweds Earle and Josephine Dickson living in New Brunswick, New Jersey, had a quandary. It seems Josephine was a bit clumsy, and every day that her husband came home from his job at Johnson & Johnson, he'd discover new cuts or burns on her fingers. Not having any kind of adhesive bandage, Earle had to cut pieces of adhesive tape and cotton gauze to bandage his wife's fingers.

One day Earle sat down and prepared some ready-made bandages for his wife, placing cotton gauze at intervals along an adhesive strip. All Josephine would have to do was cut off a piece at a time, and bandage her wound with it. Eureka.

He took his idea to his employers at Johnson & Johnson, and the idea of the "Band-Aid" soon took off. When they didn't sell very well at first, the company began giving them out free to Boy Scouts who quickly discovered just how useful the little strips could be. Today, Johnson & Johnson estimates that their company has sold over 100 billion Band-Aids.

Band-Aid Milestones

1920: Band-Aids first appear on the American market. Only $3,000 worth are sold the first year.

1924: Band-Aid produces the first machine-made adhesive, sterilized bandage.

165

1940: The little red string used to open Band-Aid packages first appears.

1942: Millions of adhesive bandages are sent overseas to help with the war effort.

1951: Band-Aid plastic strips are first introduced.

1956: The first decorated Band-Aid appears.

1963: The Mercury astronauts take Band-Aids into space, for the first time.

1997: Band-Aids go high tech: the first Band-Aids formulated with an antibiotic ointment appear.

Take Five: Some of What Our Kids Suffer with Every Day

1. Allergies: 12 percent suffer regularly from respiratory allergies.
2. Asthma: 11 percent of American children have been diagnosed with some form of asthma.
3. Hay Fever: 10 percent have to deal with hay fever on a regular basis.
4. Learning Disabilities: 8 percent struggle with a learning disability.
5. Attention Deficit Disorder (ADD): 6 percent have been diagnosed with some form of ADD.

Take Five: Top Five Ailments Suffered by Babies

1. Jaundice

This condition, recognizable by the yellowing of the wee one's skin pigment, affects about half of all new babies. It is the result of an immature liver being unable to properly filter the bloodstream. It generally goes away with no need for treatment, but can be treated by exposing the baby to some sunlight.

2. Spitting Up

This common and frustrating problem occurs because in about half of all newborns, the valve at the top of the stomach has not closed properly. By the time baby is one year old, this usually ceases to be a problem. Smaller feedings, upright feedings, and avoiding putting pressure on baby's tummy can help.

3. Rashes

About 30 percent of babies develop "baby acne," small red bumps on the face. It should clear up (until the kid reaches his or her teens at least!). Keeping skin clean and dry alleviates the condition. Diaper rash afflicts about 35 percent of babies and should be dealt with immediately. Changing baby often, washing tushies with warm soapy water, allowing baby to go al fresco a few hours each day, avoiding plastic pants, and using a protective cream or jelly can go far to alleviate this pain in the rear rash.

4. Dehydration

Young babies can become dehydrated without warning, the result of diarrhea, vomiting, or not getting enough milk. If you suspect dehydration (if baby is crying without tears, is cool and pale, listless, has a rapid pulse, has sunken eyes or a sunken soft spot, or is only peeing once every eight hours or so) you should call your health care provider.

5. Diarrhea

A number of things can cause this smelly problem, from food allergies to diet to medications to infections. The best treatment is to provide your baby with lots of fluid.

Royal Moms

"My children are not royal; they just happen to have the Queen for their aunt." —Princess Margaret

Motherhood is a challenging enough profession—imagine also having empires to build, court revolts to put down, philandering husbands to contend with, and wars to fight. Motherhood may be the ultimate balancing act, only in this balancing act hung the fates of nations.

Wu Hou

Confucianism dictated that having women in positions of power was unnatural, which, of course, makes the journey of Wu Hou in seventh-century China even more remarkable. She rose from a thirteen-year-old concubine to the emperor Tai Tsung to eventually the position of ruler, then becoming the only women emperor in Chinese history.

By the time Wu Hou arrived at the emperor's court, she already knew how to play music, write, and had read all of the Chinese classics. When emperor Tai Tsung died in 649, Wu Hou had already entered into intimate relations with the heir, emperor Kao Tsung.

Custom dictated, though, that she retire to a Buddhist convent to mourn the loss of the deceased emperor. It was here that she was visited by the new emperor, who eventually had her brought back to the palace to be his own favorite concubine.

No Rival

She smartly eliminated her female rivals within the palace, including leading concubines and eventually the existing empress. She accused Kao Tsung's wife, Empress Wang, of killing Wu's newborn daughter. Kao Tsung believed Wu, and replaced Empress Wang to marry Wu Hou.

Within five years of her marriage, Emperor Kao Tsung suffered a crippling stroke and Empress Wu Hou immediately took over administrative duties of the court, creating in the process a secret police force to spy on her opposition. She brokered no dissent, jailing or killing anyone who stood in her way, including the unfortunate Empress Wang.

In addition, Wu Hou saw to it that all the elder statesmen who were loyal to T'ai Tsung were eliminated. She had them dismissed, exiled, or executed.

Politics

In the name of her disabled husband, she governed the empire, and she eventually won the regard of the royal court. When her husband finally did pass on, it meant that power reverted to his son (by a previous empress), Chung Tsung. The new emperor, and especially his wife, sought to replicate her success. It was clear they could not do so, so Wu Hou had them replaced by her second son, but the power was clearly back in her hands. Six years later, at the retiring age of sixty-five, she claimed the throne for herself. The decision was accepted without incident—testimony to the high regard in which she was held by the people.

Eleanor of Aquitaine

Eleanor of Aquitaine was one of the great players on the stage of feudal Europe. Born in 1122, she married two kings, having with them ten children and earning her the title of first mother, then later grandmother, to all of Europe.

Eleanor of Aquitaine married Louis VII of France at age fifteen, the year her father died. She brought with her one of the largest domains in all of present-day France. Beautiful and full of youthful vigor, she was instrumental in coaxing Louis to take on the Second Crusade. More than that, she insisted on accompanying the troops to care for the wounded.

France

The new King and Queen of France did not travel well together, and by the time they returned to France after the Crusade, they did so on separate vessels. Although they had a brief reconciliation, the marriage was annulled. Under feudal custom, all of Eleanor's land reverted to her and it wasn't long before other suitors came calling, most notably the future King Henry II of England.

With Henry she had five boys and three girls, whose eventual marriages formed an interlocking web that encompassed most of present-day Europe. Two of her sons, Richard The Lion-Heart and John Lackland, became Kings of England.

Eleanor was not only actively involved in the administration of her realm, she also presided over one of the most dynamic courts of medieval Europe. Here she encouraged the troubadours, and became a patron to two of the most dominant poetic movements of her time.

Like her marriage with Louis VII, cracks began to show in her marriage to Henry II. One theory was that Eleanor had grown fed up with Henry's infidelities and therefore led three of her sons to rebel against him. The revolt was not successful, however, and for the next fifteen years, fifty-year-old Eleanor spent her time as a captive.

Revival

It was not to be the last we would hear of her, however. Upon Henry's death, she was freed and immediately began preparing for her son Richard's ascension to the throne. Richard's preoccupation with the Crusades meant she was firmly in charge now, and she thwarted plan after plan to steal the throne from Richard.

When Richard was captured by the Duke of Austria on his return from the east, she collected his ransom and went in person to escort him to England, increasing her reputation as an extremely able politician. At almost seventy, Eleanor rode over the Pyrenees to collect the candidate chosen to be Richard's wife, (Berengaria, the daughter of King Sancho, the Wise of Navarre), bringing her eventually to Sicily where Richard married in 1191.

Richard did not produce an heir, though, and her son John was crowned king. In one of her last political acts, she traveled to Spain to collect her thirteen-year-old granddaughter, Blanche of Castile, to become the bride of Louis VIII of France, the grandson of her first husband Louis VII, closing the circle and cementing a web of alliances that would play out in Europe for centuries.

She died in 1204 at the monastery at Fontevrault, Anjou, where she had sought solace many times before. Her beauty and pique, maturity and sophistication had now played out on the world stage for eight decades.

Queen Isabella

Complicated childhood is more the norm than the exception in royal households, and certainly that of Queen Isabella I of Spain qualifies. Her half-brother, Henry IV, was made king when her father died in 1454. Three years later, a suspicious Henry IV had Isabella and her brother, Alfonso, brought to his court so they might be used as pawns by opposition nobles looking to end his reign.

As it turns out Henry IV had every right to be suspicious. When his first marriage ended in divorce and without children, Henry IV quickly remarried, this time producing an heir, a daughter, Juana. That didn't wash with the nobility. They claimed his daughter was actually the daughter of the duke of Albuquerque and they set about replacing Henry with Isabella's brother, Alfonso.

In a bloody confrontation that lasted four years, Henry IV defeated the nobles, culminating when Alfonso died of poison. Looking for a standard bearer, the nobles looked to Isabella, but she refused. All was not lost for the nobles, however, when they managed to get Henry IV to agree to accept Isabella as his successor.

Ferdinand

When Isabella married Ferdinand of Portugal in October 1469, she did so without Henry IV's approval, and Henry quickly withdrew his promise to name Isabella as the next monarch. It prompted yet another war of succession, but in 1479 the matter was settled and Isabella was recognized as queen. Henry's daughter, Juana, would spend the rest of her life in a convent.

Isabella's reign was characterized by a number of great triumphs and tragedies. The biggest tragedy was the institution of the Inquisition, which had the effect of chasing all non-Catholics, particularly Jews and Muslims, from her territories, robbing the country of much of its vibrancy.

But Queen Isabella was a leader in fostering the love of study. When she was a grown woman she devoted herself to the study of Latin, and became an important collector of books. She was extremely involved in the education of her five children (Isabella, John, Joan, Maria, and Catherine). In order to educate Prince John with ten other boys, she formed a school in her palace. Her daughters also attained a degree of education higher than was usual during this time period. This dedication to education encouraged learning in the universities and among the nobles, but importantly it also encouraged learning among women.

Columbus

Although she could not have known the magnitude of it then, one of Isabella's greatest achievements was the recognition of the possibilities represented by the mission of Christopher Columbus. As it turns out, much of Spain's good fortune would be tied to discoveries in the New World.

When Isabella died, her only heir was Joan, who was considered insane. Young Prince John died in youth, and Catherine had the misfortune to marry King Henry VIII. When she died, she left a will, a document that historians have pored over now for centuries. The will not only attests to her intelligence and savvy, it shows a sympathy and empathy for the native Americans that Columbus had brought back to Spain as slaves. The will asked her successors to treat the Indians as they would treat any of her other subjects.

Mbande Nzinga

Seventeenth century Angolan queen Mbande Nzinga had a simple way to get around a tradition that only allowed her people to be led by a king. She simply had her subjects call her king.

✦

Born to the King of Ndong, Nzinga was forced to play second fiddle to her incompetent brother after her father died. It was a period of great upheaval because of the slave trade. The Portuguese were the prime slave traders in the area of present day Angola. After years of bloody battle and pillage, Nzinga was sent by her brother to attempt to negotiate a peace with the Portuguese.

Even though the Portuguese governor showed her no respect—not even providing her with a chair—she trumped him when she showed him she was his equal by having one of the people who accompanied her kneel down for her to sit on. Despite her refusal to pay tribute to the Portuguese king, she concluded what she thought was a peaceful treaty that would stop the bloodshed.

Queen to King

When it became clear that the Portuguese had no intention of living up to the treaty, she urged her brother to rally the army and fight. He refused, so she took it upon herself to fight the Portuguese. She did it by marrying a chief from an adjacent area, conquered another kingdom, and formed astute alliances with at least four other kingdoms.

She played a vital role in the resistance to the Portuguese, personally leading her troops into battle and developing battle plans. She also gave new roles to women. Many of her bodyguards were female and women were expected to fight the Portuguese just like the men.

Nzinga was a skilled tactician, organizing her forces in the jungle and then attacking the enemy in ambushes. Among her own people, it is said, she displayed such astuteness that she amazed her subjects with her ability to recount the details of people lives.

Ultimately, though, the war with the Portuguese was one that could not be won. Her husband's tribe eventually betrayed her, but even then she was able to negotiate an alliance with the Dutch. All that did, however, was buy six more years of independence. Now in her sixties, she had fought the Portuguese almost all of her adult life.

In 1659, she was forced to sign a treaty with the Portuguese. She would spend the remaining years of her life (she lived to her eighties) to help resettle former slaves and to rebuild what remained of her kingdom. She was what she said she was, a king and mother to her people.

❀

Nur Jahan

The great seventeenth century Mughal Dynasty in India spanned two decades and bore the stamp of a young immigrant girl from the small town in the Persian empire.

The woman who later became known as Nur Jahan was born into an aristocratic Persian family. At seventeen, she married a Persian soldier, with whom she a daughter, before he was killed in battle at an early age. She later moved to the Indian court to serve as a lady-in-waiting to one of sultan's court women.

Despite being well into her thirties, as soon as the sultan, Jahangir, first spied her it was love at first sight. Within two months they were married and he gave her the title Nur Jahan, meaning "Light of the World."

She and her husband presided over a court that included victorious peace and allowed an uncharacteristic degree of religious freedom. They allowed, for example, Jesuits to challenge Muslims and to debate publicly and make converts.

The Family

Nur Jahan circumvented the conventions of the day. She delegated to people she could trust to do her bidding. Make no mistake about it, though, she approved all orders and appointments, and sanctioned who received promotions and demotions within the government.

She went to bat for women, giving land and dowries to orphan girls. Fashion was influenced by Nur Jahan, and women's clothing for the first time was modified to take into account the hot weather.

She also presided over a period of increased trade with Europe and beyond. She owned ships and opened the court at Agra to a level of commerce that had not been seen before. The city became cosmopolitan and served as a beacon of commerce and possibilities.

Poet

Nur Jahan's love of poetry translated itself into a tradition of poetry contests in the Mughal court. During the contests, the poets sparred back and forth, competing with each other. Combined with her husband's love of painting, the court at Agra became know as center for the arts, with an influence on everything from fashion and fabric to pottery, painting and poetry.

The struggle for power and influence after the death of her husband was not one Nur Jahan could win, however. When Jahangir's third son, Shah Jahan (he later built the Taj Mahal for his favorite wife, Mumtaz Mahal), became the eventual victor, her fate was sealed.

She was exiled to Lahore, where at least she could spend time with her daughter. When she died, she was buried where she wanted to be…beside her husband in a tomb that is still visible today. She was a woman ahead of her time and a pivotal figure in the history of her realm.

American Royalty: Princess Grace

The third of four children born to John and Margaret Kelly of Philadelphia, Grace Kelly was a legitimate big screen star before she became known to the world as Princess Grace. An adoring American public saw her life as a fairy tale and adopted her as a link to a long ago past that included kings and princes. Before the royal court, Kelly's royal presence was in the theater, and later on the silver screen.

In July 1949, as a twenty year old, she made a professional acting debut in a small Pennsylvania playhouse. From there she worked in the nascent television industry before landing on the big screen in *Fourteen Hours* in 1951. In 1952, the big time arrived when she landed a role in *High Noon* opposite Gary Cooper.

Oscar

It was the beginning of a meteoric rise for the Philadelphia debutante. Soon she was starring opposite Clark Gable, the most famous leading man of his generation. Alfred Hitchcock would soon come calling, casting her in a number of films. In 1954, she would win an Oscar for a dressed-down role in *The Country Girl*.

In a foreshadowing of what would later happen to her, Kelly made the 1955 movie, *The Swan*, a story about a beautiful young woman who marries a prince. What the world was to find out was that in 1954, Prince Rainier Grimaldi and Kelly met at Cannes. In the next two years there ensued a whirlwind courtship that took place on two continents. In January 1956, they announced their engagement, and in April they married.

The marriage was dubbed the "Wedding of the Century," and would be watched by more than thirty million people around the world. Kelly arrived in Monaco aboard the USS Constitution, which in turn was met by Prince Rainier's yacht. The marriage marked the beginning of family life for Kelly and the official end to her career on the silver screen.

Heir to the Throne

In the first three years, she gave birth to two children, Caroline and Albert, quickly establishing an heir to the throne. In 1965, she would add another family member, Stephanie, to the royal household.

Fairy tales, though, are just that, fairy tales. She was now alone—away from her country, away from her family, and away from her career. There were difficulties with her new husband's family. In 1960, her father died and then her husband vetoed a return to film in Hitchcock's *Marnie*. She also had several miscarriages and by the early 1970s it was clear that the couple had grown apart.

Grace was a doting mother. Despite attempts at giving her children a normal childhood, that was virtually impossible in the privilege of the royal court of Monaco. She tried to see to it that her children knew of their American heritage and they often spent summer vacations on the other side of the Atlantic.

All My Children

The normalcy Kelly attempted to bring to her children didn't stop their recklessness. At age twenty, Caroline married then quickly divorced Phillipe Junot, a man almost twenty years her senior. As a seventeen year old Stephanie told her mother she was going to follow her boyfriend to racecar-driving school.

As Kelly approached middle and late middle-age, she began to take solace in her charities, taking over as president of the American Red Cross. In 1976, she attended the Edinburgh Festival as a poetry reader and later narrated a documentary about a ballet school in Russia. She was beginning to find her creative step again when tragedy struck.

In September 1982, Princess Grace was driving Stephanie back to the Palace in Monaco and had a stroke behind the wheel. She lost control of the car and it plunged off the road down a steep embankment. Kelly was seriously injured and fell into a coma. The next day her husband and children decided to remove her life support. The memory of Grace Kelly endures in the American and public consciousness as one of style, grace, and dignity.

Queen Elizabeth I

When her Majesty Queen Elizabeth I, The Queen Mother, died in March 2002 at the age of 101, the nation and people around the world mourned. To the people of the United Kingdom, she had made the transition from mother to grandmother to great -grandmother without a hitch.

The Queen Mother began life as Elizabeth Angela Marguerite Bowes-Lyon, a commoner and the ninth of ten children. Although her father was a descendant of the Duke of Portland, a lineage that would allow him and his wife the title of Lord and Lady Strathmore, his vicar's income along with bequeathals simply wasn't enough to allow a lifestyle normally associated with the titled class.

With the outbreak of World War I, the family's summer estate in Scotland was turned into a military hospital for wounded soldiers. Little did the future Queen Mother know that this experience would provide a crucial link in her role as the mother to a nation in the next world war.

Suitors

Young Elizabeth had her fair share of suitors, most notable among them James Stuart, a not-so-well-heeled descendant of the illegitimate half-brother of Mary, Queen of Scots. The fact that he was a well-known womanizer did not stop Elizabeth from falling in love with him. Alas, though, he was finessed into going to Oklahoma to seek fame and fortune in the oil fields.

Enter shy, stuttering Prince Albert, the Duke of York, the second son of King George V. Perhaps because they had known each other since childhood and were too familiar, young Elizabeth twice rejected proposals from Prince Albert, before finally agreeing to marry him in 1923.

The quiet, retiring couple were thrust into the limelight when Prince Albert's brother, King Edward VIII abdicated the throne. On the eve of World War II, the couple, now with two daughters (the present Queen Elizabeth II and Princess Margaret), moved to Buckingham Palace to assume their duties as monarchs.

Country at War

The new Queen earned the respect of the people forever when she refused categorically to leave London under Nazi bombing. "The Princesses cannot go without me. I cannot go without the King. And the King will never leave," she famously said, even in the wake of an uncertain victory. Instead she would show up at the carnage wreaked by the enemy, consoling those who had lost loved ones and all that they had owned.

With an Allied victory in the Great War, the royal household enjoyed a well-deserved break from the devastation of the previous seven years. But just as the world was about to embark on a period of prosperity and peace, the Queen lost her husband to a stroke. In an instant, she was a widow, and her daughter, Elizabeth, the new Queen.

Queen Mom

Although she had planned to withdraw from public life forever, she was cajoled by Winston Churchill to take on a more public role. The role was uncharted territory, but for almost fifty years after her husband's death, she filled it such aplomb that it may be said she invented it.

With her grandchildren, especially Prince Charles, she took on the role of mother and confidant. When the Queen was away on foreign tours, some lasting up to six months, it was to the Queen Mother that the young prince turned. Whether it was helping Charles cope with boarding school, or helping to arrange the courtship of Diana, she was a central figure in his life.

When she died in 2002, the whole nation mourned. She had persevered through two world wars and, in an environment of declining respect for the monarchy, she remained a figure to whom steadfast respect was shown.

Quotable Mom

"If there is anything that motherhood has taught me, it is that I am not just a mother to my two children, but to every child that I encounter. They all share the same innocence and vulnerability, and they are all precious and hold the promise of an enormous potential."
—*Queen Rania of Jordan*

Royal Quotes

"Hugs can do great amounts of good—especially for children."
—Princess Diana

*"Any sane person would have left long ago.
But I cannot. I have my sons."*
—Princess Diana

"If men had to have babies, they would only ever have one each."
—Princess Diana

Short Shrift

Despite rumors to the contrary, Queen Victoria's personal journals contain numerous accounts of her affection for her children. Public photos of the royal family taken during the time portray an unsmiling, prematurely aged mother surrounded by unhappily posed children.

Reports rarely reflected that the children were often brought to the royal parents at breakfast and lunch, and accompanied the Queen throughout many of her daily activities, including her daily carriage outings. She often wrote of her children lying quietly in her arms, dancing on her knee, and, later, sitting in her lap as she attempted to write her journal.

Princess Diana

Princess Diana's celebrity was such that to much of the world she was known as Princess Di, or simply Diana. Her marriage to Prince Charles, and later her death in a tragic automobile accident in France at the tender age of thirty-six, captivated an adoring world audience.

Diana was born into a house of privilege, Park House, a home her parents rented on Queen Elizabeth II's estate at Sandringham. Her childhood playmates would have been the present queen's younger sons, Prince Andrew and Prince Edward.

Mirror Image

Domestic bliss in the Spencer household would come to an abrupt end when Diana's parents' marriage crumbled when she was just an eight-year-old. It was a bitter and rancorous divorce and in some ways it would mirror her own life much later. Like Prince Charles, Diana's father was much older than Diana's mother.

Diana never was an academic standout at school, but even early on, at West Heath school in Kent, she picked up an award for cheerfully getting jobs done, a talent she would later demonstrate to an adoring world.

Diana attended finishing school in Switzerland before returning to London, where she renewed acquaintances with her royal and not-so-royal chums and began work as a nanny and governess, and later a kindergarten teacher.

Along Comes Charles

In London, her old playmates Prince Andrew and Edward had an older brother who may not have noticed her as a four- or five-year-old on his family estate, but he sure was noticing her now.

Diana was only nineteen and Charles, thirty-one, but for a public eager for the future king to settle down and marry, that seemed to be no problem at all.

The guessing game of would they or wouldn't they came to an end on February 24, 1981, when they announced their engagement. Just over five months later, they were married in St. Paul's Cathedral in a ceremony watched by hundreds of millions around the world.

Little over a year later, Diana produced an heir, Prince William Arthur Philip Louis of Wales, and two years later, a second child, Prince Henry Charles Albert David. The public quite simply fell in love with this new royal family, particularly Diana. She had an unusual combination of shyness, glamour, and sincerity that made her a legitimate star.

Less than five years after their marriage, though, cracks began to appear. All was not well in the royal household. Later it would be revealed that Charles went back to an old love, Camilla Parker Bowles, and Diana coped with the crumbling of her marriage by developing bulimia and beginning her own affairs.

End of a Marriage

When it was announced in 1992 that they were officially separating, it came as little surprise, but rather had about it a sense of inevitability. The divorce would become official in 1996.

Diana's celebrity was anchored by an uncanny ability to combine all the best elements of motherhood with fashion, a hybrid the world had not seen before. She was a doting mother and tireless worker for causes she believed in.

After the divorce, Diana maintained her high public profile and continued many of the activities she had earlier undertaken on behalf of charities, supporting causes as diverse as the arts, children's issues, and AIDS. She had an unprecedented popularity as a member of the royal family, both in Britain and throughout the world, and she became one of the most photographed women in the world.

All that potential came to a sudden and abrupt end in 1997. Attempting to escape the paparazzi, she and her friend, Dodi Fayed, and their driver were killed in a tunnel under the streets of Paris. The outpouring of grief around the world was genuine and unprecedented.

The media had made her part of our lives since before that walk down the aisle with Prince Charles fifteen years earlier. The public was there for the birth of her children; now they attended her funeral.

Quotable Mom

"Men never think, at least seldom think, what a hard task it is for us women to go through this very often. God's will be done, and if He decrees that we are to have a great number of children, why, we must try to bring them up as useful and exemplary members of society."
—Queen Victoria

Royal Scandals

Those Royal Children

It is almost inevitable that royal children become fodder for the tabloids. Princess Stephanie of Monaco has supplied the tabs with more than a little ink. First she married her former bodyguard, but divorced him after the tabloids caught him on camera fooling around with a former Miss Topless Belgium winner. In 1998, she had a child with a person she has refused to reveal. Next she married a former circus ringmaster, then divorced him and married a circus juggler.

Single Mom

Royals are normally extremely fussy about whom their children marry. So when Norway's Crown Prince Haakon asked Mette-Marit Tjessem Høiby, a single mother with a young son from a relationship with a man convicted of drug charges, to marry him, there were more than a few raised eyebrows in royal circles. King Harald V and Queen Sonja of Norway, however, were the very epitome of modern royals, not batting an eye and welcoming the daughter-in-law into the royal fold. In January of 2003, the young princess gave birth to Princess Ingrid Alexandra.

Princess Masako: A Mom Under Pressure

The Japanese Royal Family is an institution steeped in tradition; and these traditions have been challenged in recent years by the newest royal spouse, Princess Masako. The princess, formerly a commoner, married Japan's Crown Prince Naruhito on June 9, 1993. The daughter of a diplomat, Masako had a worldly upbringing as she lived in the United States and Russia and attended the prestigious Harvard and Oxford Universities.

Before marrying, she had a career in Japan's Ministry of Foreign Affairs. After her marriage, Masako came under close media scrutiny. As princess in a Royal family that must, according to custom, produce a male heir, Masako was under incredible pressure to bear a son and thus ensure the continuation of the royal line. In 1999, Masako and the Prince were devastated by a miscarriage, but just two years later, aided by fertility drugs, the royal couple and their subjects were thrilled by a royal birth when Masako gave birth to a girl. This baby did not relieve the pressure upon Masako to produce a son and heir.

The pressure had pushed Masako to the breaking point. In

a press release, her supportive Crown Prince husband revealed that his wife was resting in seclusion, where she was "completely exhausted" from trying to accommodate royal expectations which he believed had "nullified her career and nullified her character." Some speculate that Naruhito's spirited defense of his wife signals an attempt to reform the succession laws of the Imperial House, and to allow the couple's daughter to take the throne.

13

Mothers in Law

"If you obey all the rules you miss all the fun."
—*Katharine Hepburn*

Mothers and the Law

There is nothing more natural than motherhood. And yet, over the centuries, humans have developed rules to regulate motherhood and the place of moms in society.

Did You Know...?

Although the number of lawyers hit the one million mark in the U.S. in 2003, they are still outnumbered by moms, 75 to 1.

Moms and Divorce Courts

Of all divorced women in the United States, 87 percent are the custodial parents, according to Sage Family Studies Abstracts.

Laws Surrounding Adoption

In 1851, the first U.S. state enacted adoption legislation, and by 1929, all states had adoption laws. It was not until after WW I that "closed" adoptions, the practice of keeping the identities of birth and adoptive parents a secret, became the norm. This was intended to help the child bond to his/her new family and to avoid the stigma of illegitimacy. In the 1970s, "open" adoptions became increasingly accepted.

Spanking and the Law

Spanking, or "reasonable" corporal punishment of children by their parents or guardians is legal in all American states except Minnesota. At the same time, the paddling of children by school officials is permissible in twenty-three states.

• The federal department of education says that in 1997-98 paddles were used on students approximately 458,000 times.

• In 1979, Sweden became the first nation in the world to ban the corporal punishment of children. Since then, eight nations—all in Europe—have banned spanking.

• Most Americans support their right to spank their children. An ABC News poll found that 65 percent of adults approve of spanking and half admit that they regularly spank their children.

• Southerners are more inclined to spank, with 73 percent approving of spanking.

• Statistics do not show what percentage of moms threaten their kids with the dreaded paddle.

Strike Out Striking

April 30 is "Spank Out Day U.S.A." Initiated in 1998, the day was chosen to encourage non-violent approaches to teaching children appropriate behavior.

Moms Who Make the Law

- As of 2003, 48 of the 435 members sitting in the House of Representatives were moms.

- At the state level, only 17 percent of legislators are mothers.

- All public servants, however, have had moms.

Moms Who Break the Law

Not all moms are law-abiding citizens. And unfortunately, they don't always treat their children with maternal affection and respect.

- Around the world, 55 percent of abducted children are kidnapped by their own mothers.

- Twelve percent of children who are abused are abused by mom.

Protecting the Unborn

In recent decades, Americans have grown increasingly aware of the health risks posed to unborn babies by moms who participate in certain activities. The legal system has kept apace of new medical knowledge, and laws have been enacted to proscribe certain activities on the part of pregnant moms-to-be.

In 1989, for the first time ever, a mother in the United States was charged with a felony drug charge when she was convicted of delivering drugs to a minor—cocaine delivered through her umbilical cord to her unborn infant.

Seven years later, in 1996, a baby girl was born to Deborah Zimmerman. Tragically, something was terribly wrong with the baby and the baby died. As it turned out, the infant's blood alcohol registered a whopping .20, more than twice the legal level for operating a vehicle.

On June 10, 1996, legal history was made when Zimmerman

was charged with the first-degree intentional homicide of her daughter—a crime she committed by drinking copiously before the baby's birth. This was the first time that a mother in the U.S. was charged with this offense. Tragically, each year forty-thousand American babies are born with birth defects as a result of pre-natal alcohol exposure.

Babies Behind Bars

1,300 babies are born to moms behind bars annually, according to " Mothers Behind Bars."

BREAKING THE RULES: ROSIE O'DONNELL

Roseanne (Rosie) O'Donnell was born to Irish spy-satellite technician Edward O'Donnell and Roseanne Murtha O'Donnell on March 21, 1962 in Commack, New York. In 1973, her own mother died of breast cancer at only thirty-eight years old. Just ten years old at the time of her mom's death, Murtha's passing had a profound influence on young Rosie.

Perhaps this explains why her own motherhood is such an important personal goal, and an object of tireless activism for the much-loved comedienne and actress. Rosie's road to fame began with a well-received stand-up comedy show in the 1980s, which she quickly parlayed into a successful acting career.

Success in movies followed, and she appeared in several hits—including her portrayal of the much-loved cartoon mom, Betty Rubble, in the film adaptation of *The Flintstones*. In June 1996 her wildly popular daytime talk show, *The Rosie O'Donnell Show* hit the airwaves.

COUNT 'EM

Between 1997 and 2002, O'Donnell's show garnered six consecutive daytime Emmys with the "Queen of Nice" herself receiving five consecutive Emmys as host. In more recent years, Rosie has also succeeded on Broadway, where, in 1996, she made her debut starring as Rizzo in Grease.

Rosie has used her amazing celebrity in support of a number of causes. She has tirelessly used her celebrity to fight the disease that claimed her mother. And she has also advanced family and children's charities. Her affection and concern for the plight of children took on personal meaning when, in 1995, she adopted her first child, a son named Parker. Two more adopted children followed. In 1997, Rosie adopted daughter Chelsea, and in 1999 added a third adopted child, Blake, to the O'Donnell family.

INSPIRED

Inspired by her own status as an adoptive parent, Rosie has emerged as a stalwart supporter of the adoption cause. In 2000, Rosie's adoption activism took a new turn. That year, the state of Florida refused to allow a gay couple the right to legally adopt the HIV-positive foster son they had raised for a decade. The reason? The couple was gay. Incensed, Rosie leant her celebrity clout to the cause. For the first time, live on TV, Rosie publicly acknowledged her own homosexuality, and petitioned for an end to laws that deny gay parents the right to adopt.

In a March 2002 interview, Rosie asserted that "I don't think America knows what a gay parent looks like. I am a gay parent." She also noted that "I know I'm a really good mother. I know it. I'm a really good mother. And I have every right to parent this child."

Arizona Donnie Clark was born in 1887. In 1907, at the age of twenty, Arizona (or "Kate," as she was called), married George Barker and took the last name that would make her infamous. Kate and George had four sons: Herman, Lloyd, Arthur, and Freddie. When the boys were young, George abandoned the family and Kate was left to raise her rambunctious brood alone.

Inspired by tales of the outlaw Jesse James, the Barker boys, mischievous in their youth, grew into lawless men. The boys formed an outlaw gang, the "Barker Gang," and became professional robbers. The role of Ma Barker in her sons' criminal escapades is hotly debated to this day.

Was Ma Barker merely a devoted mom who loved her flawed, gun-toting family unconditionally? Or was she the criminal mastermind behind their dastardly deeds? There is little doubt that she loved and supported her boys.

THAT'S MY BOYS

As the four found themselves in trouble with the law time and again, Ma stood by them. She ceaselessly campaigned for their releases from their many arrests and incarcerations. In her eyes, her sons could do no wrong. Indeed, Ma Barker apparently believed that her thieving sons were unfairly targeted by police and she complained that her boys were "marked," the victims of overzealous cops who "won't ever stop persecuting my boys."

There is some suggestion that Ma Barker was also in the thick of her boys' escapades. It is widely believed that she regularly took a cut from their criminal earnings. The violent events of January 1935 seem to underscore Ma's dedication to her sons' criminality.

That winter, Ma and her youngest boy, a wanted fugitive, Fred, were vacationing in Florida when the FBI was tipped off to their location. Police surrounded their shack, calling for the mother and son duo to surrender. When police threatened that they were about to unleash tear gas on the hideout, Ma allegedly retorted "All right...go ahead!"

A machine gun battle ensued. When the hail of bullets came to an end, Ma and Fred were found dead, lying side by side. Was this horrifying end a case of a loving mother sacrificing herself for her baby boy? Or does it confirm J. Edgar Hoover's assertion that Ma Barker was "one of the most vicious, dangerous, and resourceful criminal brains" of his era?

The Favorite

Allegedly, Ma Barker's favorite was her youngest son, Fred. Apparently, this is not an uncommon phenomenon. According to a study by Cornell and Louisiana State Universities, 80 percent of moms with grown children admitted they have a favorite child. Young Freddy likely had an inkling of his mother's fondness for him, because 80 percent of children in this survey suspected that their mom has a favorite.

Take Five: Five Scary Moms

1. Diane Downs
2. Joan Crawford (*Mommy Dearest*)
3. Mrs. Bates (*Psycho*)
4. Queen Alien (*Aliens*)
5. Mrs. Lift (*Throw Momma from the Train*)

Looney Laws

- Women may not drive in a housecoat in California.   ❀

- In Wichita, Kansas, a man's mistreatment of his mother-in-law may not be used as grounds for divorce.

- In Florida, housewives are not allowed to break more than three dishes a day, or to chip the edges of more than four cups and/or saucers.

Little Known Child-Rearing Laws Every Mother Should Know

- In Oregon, babies may not be carried on the running boards of cars.

- In Tennessee it is illegal to dare a child to purchase beer. Also in Tennessee, no Christian parent may require their children to pick up trash from the highway on Easter day.

- In Mesquite, Texas, it is illegal for children to have unusual haircuts. But what constitutes "unusual" these days?

- In West Virginia, no children may attend school with their breath smelling of "wild onions." (Garlic breath is apparently okay.)

- In L.A., you cannot bathe two babies in the tub at the same time.

- If a child burps during church in Nebraska, his parents may be arrested. It is also illegal in that state for a mother to give her daughter a perm without a state license.

Biblical Laws about Moms

"And Adam called his wife's name Eve;
because she was the mother of all living."
—Genesis 3:20

"Honor thy father and thy mother: that thy days may be
long upon the land which the Lord thy God giveth thee."
—Exodus 20:12

"And he that smiteth his father, or his mother,
shall besurely put to death."
—Exodus 21:15

"And God said unto Abraham, As for Sarai thy wife,
thou shalt not call her name Sarai, but Sarah shall her name
be. And I will bless her, and give thee a son also of her: yea,
I will bless her, and she shall be a mother of all nations;
kings of people shall be of her."
—Genesis 17:15-16

"For every one that curseth his father or his mother shall be
surely put to death: he hath cursed his father or his mother;
his blood shall be upon him."
—Leviticus 20:9

"For God commanded, saying, Honor thy father and mother:
and, He that curseth father or mother, let him die the death."
—Matthew 15: 4

"My son, hear the instruction of thy father, and forsake
not the law of thy mother: For they shall be an ornament
of grace unto thy head and chains about thy neck."
—Proverbs 1:8–9

*"For I was my father's son, tender and only
beloved in the sight of my mother."*
—Proverbs 4:3

*"A wise son maketh a glad father: but a foolish man
despiseth his mother."*
—Proverbs 15:20

*"Whoso curseth his father or his mother, his lamp shall
be put out in obscure darkness."*
—Proverbs 20:20

"As one whom his mother comforts, so will I comfort you."
—Isaiah, 66:13

MARY HARRIS (MOTHER JONES), 1830-1930, CHALLENGER OF LABOR LAWS AND MOTHER

Reportedly born in Ireland in 1830, Mary Harris emigrated with her family to the United States in 1835. In 1861, she married George Jones, a prominent member of Chicago's Iron Moulder's Union.

Jones was a mother in two senses of the word. Quite literally, she mothered four children, and knew well the pain that often accompanies that job. In 1867, yellow fever tragically claimed her husband and all four of her young children. Mary Harris Jones emerged from this personal tragedy and attempted to rebuild her life by building a dress-making business in Chicago. Four years later, disaster struck again when fire destroyed her business. Alone and penniless, Mary identified with the precariousness of working class life. She turned her "mothering" to the working class of America.

In the late nineteenth century, an era renowned for industrial abuses, "Mother" Jones committed herself to organizing male and female workers to fight for their rights and challenge unscrupulous employers. Ever a thorn in the sides of wealthy business owners, Mother Jones was an outspoken labor activist and organizer at a time when American women were expected to be quiet and at home.

Perhaps in loving memory of her own lost children, Jones tirelessly crusaded against child labor. In 1903, she organized child mill and mine workers into a "Children's Crusade." Sporting banners that read "We want time to play!" and "We want to go to school!," the young protestors marched from Kensington, PA, to Oyster Bay, NY, the home of President Theodore Roosevelt.

With these and other campaigns, Mary Harris Jones catapulted the cause of child labor to the fore of American consciousness. In the 1920s, failing health forced Jones to limit her public appearances and she devoted her time to the writing of her autobiography. Mary Harris (Mother) Jones died on November 30, 1930.

Literal Mothers-In-Law

Pentheraphobia is a horrifying disorder. Thankfully, this "persistent, abnormal, and irrational fear" of one's mother-in-law is fairly rare. Regardless, mothers-in-law have gotten a bad rap over the years.

From Fred Flintstone's ceaseless war with his mother-in-law, whom he referred to as "The Battle-Axe," to Princess Di's alleged decades-long battle with her regal mother-in-law, mothers-in-law have entered the world of stereotype in the American mind.

But are mothers-in-law that bad? How do Americans and their mothers-in-law really get along? Apart from a Progressive Insurance survey that showed 38 percent of Americans who say they would rather kiss their car than kiss their mother-in-law, most Americans love their mothers-in-law and appreciate their advice and assistance.

Who Ya Gonna Call?

- Sixty-five percent of mothers-in-law can feel the love—they think that their daughters-in-law respect their advice, according to Divorce On-Line.

- Only 11 percent of mothers-in-law say that their sons-in-law or daughters-in-law don't respect their advice.

Oh Happy Days

In fact, we love our mothers-in-law so much that we have set aside a special day to celebrate them. Started in 1934 by a newspaper editor in Amarillo, Texas, Mother-in-Law Day is celebrated on the fourth Sunday in October.

SARA DELANO ROOSEVELT VS.
ELEANOR ROOSEVELT

One of the most famous mother/mother-in-law relationships was that of First Lady Eleanor Roosevelt and her mother-in-law, Sara Delano Roosevelt. It is typically asserted that Sara Roosevelt was the quintessential domineering mother-in-law who disliked her son's wife, spoiled her grandchildren, and made every effort to undermine Eleanor.

When Eleanor Roosevelt met, fell in love with, and married her fifth cousin, Franklin Delano

Roosevelt in 1905, Sara opposed the union. But early in the marriage, the two warmed up to each other and Eleanor often turned to her mother-in-law for guidance and support.

Certainly, tension often punctuated their relationship. The birth of Eleanor's six children heightened the tension between the two and differences of opinion regarding child rearing were a constant source of conflict. Sara also disapproved of Eleanor's activism and her involvement in politics, and openly shared her opinion on the matter.

FIGHTING FOR RIGHTS

Despite her mother-in-law's opposition, Eleanor had an astounding political career. She not only helped her husband win election to the White House in 1933, but she was an outspoken advocate of women's suffrage, lobbied tirelessly for wage parity for women and the implementation of child labor laws, and staunchly campaigned against racial inequity. As chair person to the 1948 Commission of Human Rights she oversaw the drafting and adoption of the Universal Declaration of Human Rights—a contribution that Eleanor herself heralded as her most important life's work.   ❀

Eleanor's private life, particularly her cool relationship with her mother-in-law, is a perplexing one. As one biographer has mused, "one of the great mysteries" of Eleanor's life is why she "could not tell her mother-in-law to mind her own business—and do so within the boundaries of a decorum to which they both adhered."

A MOM WHO CHALLENGED CIVIL RIGHTS LAWS: CORETTA SCOTT KING

Born in Marion, Alabama, Scott was her class valedictorian at Lincoln High School and went on to earn a Bachelor of Arts degree in Music and Teaching from Antioch College. Scott then moved to Boston, attended the New England Conservatory of Music, and earned a degree in voice and violin.

While there, she met Martin Luther King, Jr., and they wed on June 18, 1953. In September of 1954 the newlyweds took up residence in Montgomery, Alabama. Coretta and Martin Luther King, Jr. had four children: Martin Luther King III, Yolanda, Bernice, and Dexter.

AN ADVOCATE

Scott King devoted much of her early years to raising their children, but struck a balance between her family and civil rights activism. She worked side-by-side with her husband throughout the 1950s and 1960s. She took part in the Montgomery Bus Boycott of 1955 and worked to pass the 1964 Civil Rights Act.

Following her husband's assassination in 1968, she continued their life's work, founding the Martin Luther King, Jr. Center for Nonviolent Social Change in Atlanta. She served as the Center's president and CEO from its inception. In 1980, a twenty-three-acre site around King's birthplace was designated for use by the King Center. The following year, a museum complex was dedicated on the site.

King also was behind the fifteen-year fight to have her husband's birthday instituted as a national holiday. In 1995, King passed the reins of the King Center over to her son, Dexter, but she remains in the public eye.

She writes regular articles on social issues and publishes a syndicated column. She has also been a regular commentator on CNN since 1980. Martin Luther King III now serves as president of the Southern Christian Leadership Conference (SCLC);

Yolanda is an actress; Bernice works as a lawyer and Baptist minister; and Dexter runs the King Library and Archive. All had a great role model in their mom.

MADONNA: A MOM WHO BROKE ALL THE RULES

On August 16, 1958, Madonna Louise Ciccone was one of six children born to Silvio (Tony) Patrick Ciccone and Madonna Louise (Fortin) Ciccone. She was raised in a working-class suburb of Pontiac, Michigan. When Madonna was just five years old, her mother was diagnosed with breast cancer and died in 1963.

Her mother's death forced Madonna to grow up before her time, and a very young Madonna helped care for her younger siblings. Despite early hardships, Madonna had a pretty typical childhood and was a talented cheerleader and top student.

After a brief stint studying dance, Madonna decided to move to New York City to become a star. She once admitted, "I'm tough, I'm ambitious, and I know exactly what I want." And, indeed, she made her dreams come true. In New York, her love of dance was eclipsed by her love of singing. Early 1980s performances in the bar scene won Madonna a record deal, and in 1982 she won a video deal for her single "Everybody."

WHAT A DEBUT

A year later, Madonna released a reasonably successful debut album, but it wasn't until her second album, one that spawned the hit single "Lucky Star", that she became a sensation. Lucky or not, Madonna's star had clearly risen.

In 1984, she appeared on *American Bandstand*. Her sexy rendition of "Like a Virgin" stole the show on the first ever MTV Music Video Awards.

Madonna soon set her sites on movie-stardom. Her first real screen debut came with *Desperately Seeking Susan*, the highest grossing film of 1985. That same year, she met and fell in love with quick-tempered and quicker-fisted actor, Sean Penn. Within a few weeks they were engaged, and on Madonna's twenty-seventh birthday they married. The next fall, the newly-weds agreed to star in *Shanghai Surprise*, which was an utter box office flop. Her next movie, *Who's that Girl?*, shared the same fate.

On top of the charts, but floundering in cinemas, Madonna's married life was spinning out of control. In the mid-1980s her husband Sean waged war on the paparazzi and wound up facing assault charges, jail terms, and probation. In 1988 the rocky marriage finally came to an end.

IRREVERENT

The 1990s continued to be turbulent for Madonna as her sexy onscreen antics and irreverence won her much scorn. Her 1989 "Like a Prayer" video was lambasted for its alleged sacrilege, and the sexually explicit *Truth or Dare* documentary and *Sex*, a risqué book of photographs, ruffled even more feathers.

Now in her late thirties, Madonna was prepared for another role in life: that of mother. In 1994, while on her daily jog, Madonna met fitness instructor Carlos Leon. In April 1996, Madonna and Leon announced the impending birth of a child. On October 14, 1996, thirty-eight-year-old Madonna gave birth to Lourdes Maria Ciccone Leon. Madonna's life took a new turn, and mother-hood took center stage.

In the winter of 2000, Madonna discovered that she was pregnant again, this time by her new boyfriend, film director Guy Ritchie. On August 11, 2000, son Rocco John Ritchie was born.

Madonna took her new baby home on her forty-second birthday, and that same year, Madonna and her "soul mate" Guy Ritchie were married.

Madonna embraced her new role as wife and mother. A woman who had previously graced the cover of *Playboy* now fronted *Good Housekeeping*. Motherhood seemingly agrees with Madonna, who has remarked: "It feels to me that I'm slowly revealing myself, my true nature. It feels to me like I'm just getting close to the core of who I really am." No longer a wild "Material Girl," Madonna is a contented mom.

14

Brains, Brawn, Beauty, and Bravery: Moms with Extraordinary Talent and Conviction

A Mother of Invention

The idea for Ann Moore's invention came to her while she was serving as a Peace Corps volunteer in French West Africa. Moore had noticed mothers there carrying their babies in backpack-like contraptions. She liked the closeness between the mother and child, and hoped to be able to form a bond like that with her own baby.

When she returned home, she and her mother designed a baby carrier similar to the one she had seen while in the Peace

Corps, and the "Snugli" carrier was patented in 1969. Today, thanks to Moore's ingenuity, millions of mothers and fathers now form a bond with their infant kids while carrying them around on their backs in a Snugli!

Take Five: Five Elected Moms

1. Ann Richards

Ann Richards has served the people of Texas as a county commissioner, state treasurer, and finally, as the state's forty-fifth governor. She and her husband David Richards have four grown children.

2. Hillary Rodham Clinton

This is one political mom who should be no stranger to you. Former First Lady Hillary Clinton is currently serving as the junior senator from New York. She and her husband, former President William Jefferson Clinton, have one daughter, Chelsea.

3. Geraldine Ferraro

Geraldine Ferraro's career as a successful New York Congresswoman was overshadowed in 1984, when she became the first woman candidate chosen by a major party to run for the Vice Presidency. Ferraro's bid for executive office was unsuccessful, however, as she and her running mate, Walter Mondale, were crushed by Ronald Reagan in the election. She has three children, Donna, John, and Laura, with husband John Zaccaro.

4. Nancy Landon Kassebaum

Nancy Landon Kassebaum was the first female in the United States Senate who did not get there by succeeding a husband who died while in office. The daughter of Alfred Kassebaum, a former Governor of Kansas, Nancy seemed to have politics in her blood. She earned her Bachelor's Degree in political science from the University of Kansas, and soon found work in Republican Kansas Senator James Pearson's office. When Pearson decided to retire from public service in 1978, Kassebaum went for his job and won, capturing 55 percent of the vote. She represented the people of Kansas for almost twenty years, before retiring in 1997. She is married to former Tennessee Senator Howard Baker, and has three children from a previous marriage.

5. Diane Feinstein

A well-known politician, Diane Feinstein has a reputation for breaking down barriers. She was the first female mayor of San Francisco and the first female Senator elected from California. Feinstein has one daughter, Katherine.

Quotable Mom

"When Chelsea Victoria Clinton lay in my arms for the first time, I was overwhelmed by the love and responsibility I felt for her. Despite all the books I had read, all the children I had studied and advocated for, nothing prepared me for the sheer miracle of her being." —Hilary Rodham Clinton, I Love Being a Mom: Treasured Stories, Memories and Milestones

Million Mom March

In late 1999, Donna Dees-Thomases, a New Jersey mother of two and stepmother of three, was horrified by recent shooting sprees that targeted children. Believing that moms had to respond to this violence, in September 1999, Dees-Thomases and twenty-five like-minded moms announced their solution to the epidemic of children-related gun violence.

At a news conference she announced that a grassroots

movement of mothers, called the Million Mom March and modeled after Mothers Against Drunk Driving, would march on Washington on Mother's Day 2000, a symbolic nine months later. On May 14, 2000, 750,000 marchers convened on the National Mall in Washington, DC, and were joined by an additional 150,000–200,000 marchers across the nation.

The agenda of the Million Mom March was to lobby Congress to implement gun laws that will keep weapons out of the hands and lives of children in America. In 2001, the Million Mom March merged with the Brady Campaign to Prevent Gun Violence, and together the two organizations continued to lobby for laws preventing gun violence. The Million Mom March continues to be a strong force in America, buoyed by the fact that between its first march in 2000 and its third in 2003, 13,000 American children and teens in America were killed by firearms.

Quotable Mom

"If we moms can push nine pound babies through our bodies, some of them with heads as big as bowling balls, surely we can push legislation through the halls of Congress."
—Donna Dees-Thomases, founder of the Million Mom March

World Leader Moms

Margaret Thatcher

Margaret Thatcher became the first female European Prime Minister when she was elected PM of Great Britain in 1979—a position she would hold for eleven years. During her time at 10 Downing Street, Thatcher was at the helm of major economic reform akin to Ronald Reagan's "supply side" economic agenda.

The economy was only part of her mandate. In 1982 she led Britain to war with Argentina for control of the Falkland Islands. Her stern economic policies and firm resolve over Falkland Islands earned Thatcher the not quite flattering nickname the "Iron Lady." Eventually, Thatcher's economics lead to her political downfall. Thatcher opposed the economic unification of Europe, but most of her colleagues did not. Margaret Thatcher and her husband Denis have twins, a son Mark and a daughter Carol.

Indira Gandhi

As the only child of Kamla and Jawaharlal Nehru, Indira Gandhi was destined for a career in politics. Her father, a friend and colleague of Mohandas Gandhi and a supporter of the struggle for Indian independence, served as the country's first Prime Minister.

Indira followed in her father's footsteps. She was first elected to the Indian parliament in 1964, and within two years, had become the country's third Prime Minister and the first female leader of the country. Initially she was wildly popular in India, but an economic recession led to calls for her dismissal and in 1977 her Congress party was defeated, her political career seemingly over.

Just three years later, she was again elected Prime Minister. Her hard line on Sikh secessionists, however, won her many enemies and on Halloween of 1984, Indira was assassinated by two Sikh members of her own bodyguard. She had two children. Her youngest son Sanjay was killed in a plane crash in 1977. Her older son, Rajiv, was sworn in as head of the Congress Party and Prime Minister of India following her death, thereby continuing the political tradition of his grandfather and mother.

Golda Meir

Former Israeli Prime Minister Golda Meir was born in Kiev, Ukraine, in 1898. Her family emigrated to America, first to Milwaukee and later to Denver. In Denver she met her future husband, Morris Meyerson, whom she married upon turning nineteen (she eventually changed her name from Meyerson to Meir in the mid-1950s in order to make it more Hebrew sounding).

Following the wedding, the couple emigrated to Palestine, and then to Jerusalem. There, Golda gave birth to two children: Menachem and Sarah. Life as a housewife did not sit well with Golda and she took a job as a secretary of a labor group in 1928. Her political career had begun, and it put a burden on her family. She and Morris eventually separated, though they never formally divorced.

In 1946, Golda became head of the Jewish Agency's Political Department and when the state of Israel was established in 1948, it was Golda who went to the United States to solicit money to arm the new nation. Meir held many posts in the new Israeli government, but Meir is best known for her stint as Israeli Prime Minister. When Prime Minister Levi Eshkol died in 1969, the seventy-one-year-old Meir assumed the position, becoming only the third female Prime Minister in history. Meir resigned in 1974 in favor of Yitzhak Rabin. She died in 1978.

Sadly, Golda felt that her dedication to Israeli politics had not only cost her marriage, but that it took time away from her mothering her children. Despite their mother's misgivings, both of Meir's children had happy lives. Menachem would grow up to become a cellist, while Sarah became a kibbutznik.

Mary Robinson

Born May 21, 1944, in Dublin Ireland, Mary Robinson would become the first female President of Ireland. She received her early schooling in Ireland, and earned a law degree from Trinity

College, Dublin. She then traveled to Boston to attend Harvard Law School, where she received a Master of Law degree with first class standing. This achievement allowed the twenty-five-year-old Robinson to return to Ireland, where in 1969 she became the country's youngest ever law professor. That same year, Robinson was elected to the Upper House of the Irish Parliament, a position she held for twenty years until she was elected President in 1990.

As President of Ireland, Robinson took an active interest in world affairs, and tried to draw attention to global crises. She was the first western leader to visit famine-ravaged Somalia, and was also the first to visit Rwanda following the genocide that occurred there. Mary Robinson resigned as President of Ireland on September 12, 1997. She is married to Nicholas Robinson, and has three children: Theresa, William, and Aubrey.

Vigdis Finnbogadottir

Here's a name that might be unfamiliar to you, but it is well-known in Iceland. Born April 15, 1930, in Reykjavik, Iceland, Vigdis Finnbogadottir was the world's first democratically elected female leader, winning her home country's presidency in 1980. For sixteen years, President Vigdis (Icelanders tend not to use last names) was head of state for the island nation, and was by far its most popular politician. She was reelected in 1984, 1988, and 1992 with overwhelming majorities. In fact, she won one election with an astonishing 93 percent of the vote! Perhaps the only thing keeping her from still being Iceland's President is that she declined to re-offer in 1996. She has one daughter, whom she adopted prior to beginning her political career.

Take Five: Five Media Moms

1. Barbara Walters

A co-anchor of 20/20 and a member of *The View*, this multiple Emmy winner is known for making celebrities cry during their interviews with her on her Barbara Walters Specials. Walters has a daughter, Jacqueline, with ex-husband Lee Gruber.

2. Katie Couric

Another multiple Emmy winner, Couric has been co-anchor of NBC's *Today Show* since 1991. She was also the recipient of the 2002 "WOW Woman of the Year" award by *Glamour* magazine. She has two daughters, Elinor and Caroline, with her late husband.

3. Maria Shriver

Now perhaps best known for being the First Lady of California and the wife of Governor Arnold Schwarzenegger, Shriver also has a lengthy career in broadcasting under her belt. This former host of NBC's *Weekend Nightly News* and *Dateline* has won both an Emmy award and a Peabody award. She and Ah-nold have four children.

4. Lesley Stahl

Lesley Stahl is currently a co-anchor on the hit show *60 Minutes*, and a former moderator of the news discussion show *Face the Nation*, for which she has won several Emmy awards. She has also won the prestigious Dennis Kauff Journalism Award for lifetime achievement in the news profession. Stahl and her husband Aaron Lathom have one daughter, Taylor.

5. Christiane Amanpour

Christiane Amanpour is CNN's Chief International Correspondent. From her London base, Amanpour travels throughout Europe and Asia, to the world's trouble spots. She has seen firsthand the horrors of Rwanda, the tragedy of Bosnia, and most recently has been filing reports from Iraq. Amanpour has received multiple awards for her efforts, including a pair of Emmys and a pair of Peabodys.

Christine Amanpour is married to ex-U.S. State Department spokesman Jamie Rubin, with whom she has one son, Darius. The arrival of her child prompted Amanpour to feel a greater obligation to "stay alive," but she still remains dedicated to journalism. Said Amanpour after her son's birth, "Lately I've been wondering why I do it, why anyone would do it. The answer used to come after only a few seconds: because it matters, because the world will care once people see our stories. Because if the storytellers don't do this, then the bad people will win."

MARIE CURIE

Marie Curie was born Marie Sklodowski on November 7, 1867, in Warsaw, Poland. Both teachers, her parents emphasized their children's education. Although Marie excelled at school, careers for educated women were almost non-existent in Poland, as women were forbidden to attend university. Undaunted, Marie and her sister decided to move to Paris where Marie worked to support the pair while her sister attended medical school. After her sister's graduation, the tables turned and Marie herself attended Paris' prestigious Sorbonne, enrolling as one of the very few women in the School of Science. After graduating with a Masters degree in physics, she completed her Masters in Mathematics.

PHYSICS

Soon thereafter, Marie met a brilliant young physicist who would change her life. Marie and Pierre Curie fell in love and were married in 1895. For the next fourteen years, the happy and brilliant couple studied the emerging phenomenon of radioactive substances. But Marie did more than just discover radioactive material; she also explained the origins of radioactivity, explaining that it was an atomic phenomenon, and did not occur at the molecular level as was previously thought.

This was a revolutionary theory as not all turn of the century scientists were convinced that atoms even existed! But Marie was correct, and in 1903 she, Pierre, and a colleague received the Nobel Prize in Physics for their discovery.

In addition to being the "mother of the atomic age," Marie was also the mother of Irene, a baby girl born in 1897. But Marie's motherhood experience was not without tragedy. In 1903, the year she received her greatest scientific recognition, she also received her greatest heartbreak. She suffered a miscarriage, probably as a result of exposure to radiation. Still, Marie did not give up on motherhood, and in 1904 she gave birth to another healthy girl, Eve. Two years later, in 1906, tragedy again struck the Curies when Pierre was killed when run over by a carriage.

SORBONNE

Following Pierre's death, the Sorbonne appointed Marie to Pierre's professorship in physics and Marie became the first woman in France to hold this prestigious position. But this was small consolation for a woman wracked by grief. Marie found solace in fellow physicist, Paul Langevin and their friendship soon escalated into a romantic affair—something Langevin's wife was less than thrilled about.

She intercepted love letters exchanged by the couple, and threatened to publish them. Indeed, some made it to press and Marie was scandalized. When Marie won a second Nobel Prize, she was asked not to attend the ceremony in the wake of the scandal. Marie defied the academy's wishes, and in 1911 showed up to pick up her prize.

During the early years of her scientific career, Marie saw little of her girls. They spent most of their time in the care of their grandfather. As the children grew older, however, Marie became a more integral part of their lives. She encouraged them, and helped them to achieve their dreams. Like her mother, Irene Curie would also receive a Nobel Prize in chemistry for her own work on artificial radiation.

A Tough Mom's Tough Love

Usually we frown on parents kidnapping children, but in this case an exception might be warranted. In order to save her daughter Desirée Danner from an eight-hundred-dollars-a-day cocaine habit, mom Brenda Romero kidnapped her and took her home for forcible detoxification. The windows were screwed shut, the doors were dead-bolted, and Desirée wasn't allowed outside without at least two family member escorts. Although it usually takes the body a week to detoxify itself from drugs, Brenda kept her daughter for twenty-one days just to be safe.

At first Desirée wasn't too keen on the situation; she fought her mother and threatened that once released she would never see her mom again. But Brenda's resolve didn't waver. And Desirée's anger did. She and her mother now have a close relationship, and Desirée works as a counselor in a rehab center. As to why she intervened so forcefully in her daughter's life, Brenda says "I kidnapped my daughter because she was at her lowest point before death, and I couldn't risk her caring for herself on her own."

Winning Moms

Women athletes are no longer expected to abandon sports when their children arrive. In fact, some of the best athletes in the world are moms, and increasingly, top-ranking sporting organizations are respecting women's desires for family and their desires to win. Consider the Women's National Basketball Association. The WNBA offers maternity leave to its players, and in 2000 there were sixteen moms on its roster of 132 players. The U.S. Soccer Federation pays a nanny to care for the children of the two moms on the U.S. team.

Quotable Mom

"My son thinks it's so cool and so exciting that his mom is a professional basketball player."
—Suzie McConnell Serio,
WNBA Player, the Cleveland Rockers.

"Sometimes I worry if I'm doing the right thing by bringing [my son] along and dragging him from country to country"
—Carla Overbeck, World Cup Soccer Player

"IRON MOM" KAREN SMYERS

The Ironman triathlon is one of the most grueling sports imaginable. And one of America's best Ironman athletes is not a man at all—she is a mother of two! Karen Smyers competed in her first triathlon in 1984 and has been one of America's top tri-athletes ever since. But her successful career, marred by obstacles and tragedies, has not been easy.

Her bad luck began with a string of accidents in 1997. In June of that year, just one day before she was scheduled to compete at the ITU World Cup in Monte Carlo, she severed her hamstring in an accident at home. Undaunted, Smyers and her husband, movie producer Michael King, used her recovery time to start their family. Baby Jenna was born on May 1, 1998 in a long and difficult labor, ended by a Cesarean section. Of her labor, Smyers remarked, "I'd do ten Ironmans in a row before going through that labor again."

BACK AT IT

Amazingly, less than three months later, Smyers competed in a triathlon. But there were more challenges to come her way. In August 1998, Smyers was training for the Ironman when she was hit by a semi-truck. Suffering broken ribs, a lung contusion, and a shoulder separation, Smyers missed the 1998 season. Believing she was on the road to recovery, Smyers was sideswiped again—this time by a cancer diagnosis. But before she would have her cancerous thyroid removed, Smyers insisted on competing in the Hawaiian Ironman competition. Two days after the race, she had her surgery.

As she had won so many races, so too did Smyers beat cancer, and is again competing in her sport. Says Smyers of her sport, "It's just a part of who I am and what makes me tick." Her family also makes her tick. Of her first birth ordeal with her daughter, Smyers said "It definitely was not my dream birth, and I was absolutely convinced she would be an only child after going through that." But as Smyers, of all people knows, memories of labor pain fade. In early 2004 she gave birth to her second child, a son.

Golfing Mom

"The girls understand that my job is different from the other moms' jobs, but they're very proud of what I do and they still enjoy coming with me, which is great. They'll come home and say one of their friends wants me to sign something, and they just laugh. Or we'll be having dinner somewhere and someone will walk by and say, 'Hi, Juli' and they wonder how people know my name. They sometimes have a hard time grasping it, but as far as they're concerned, I'm their mom and everyone at school knows I'm just Hayley and Cori's mom." —Juli Inkster, LPGA Champion

FIGURE SKATER EKATERINA GORDEEVA

Born on May 28, 1971, in Moscow, it was evident even when she was a little girl in Russia that Ekaterina Gordeeva would be a world class skater. At age eleven, Ekaterina met her new skating pairs partner, a handsome fifteen-year-old named Sergei Grinkov. The two skated together for thirteen years, and excelled at their sport, winning Olympic medals at the 1984 and 1988 games. Not only that, but the two fell in love and were married in 1991. In 1992 the couple had their daughter, Daria; life, it seems, could not have been better for the new parents.

In 1995, tragedy struck. During a practice session, twenty-eight-year-old Sergei suffered a fatal heart attack, leaving his twenty-four-year-old wife a widow and a single mom. Though lost without her beloved husband, Ekaterina persevered, buoyed by her passion for skating and especially by her young daughter, whom she calls the accomplishment of which she is most proud. After her husband's death, Ekaterina continued her career, wowing audiences with her Stars on Ice performances.

Ekaterina is, however, above all, a devoted mom. She shows her adoration and love for her daughter as she shares childhood memories and Russian culture in a book called *A Letter for Daria*. Ekaterina cherishes her daughter more than anything, and has commented that "Any time spent with Daria is enjoyable. It doesn't matter what we do."

Quotable Mom

"She (Daria) has Sergei's wide and ready smile, so beautiful to me."
—Ekaterina Gordeeva, Olympic figure skater

Take Five: Five Athletic Moms

1. Steffi Graf

German born tennis star Steffi Graf was one of the most dominant female players ever to play the game. She is married to another hero of the hard court, American ace Andre Agassi. Together, the athletic couple have served up a pair of children: a son, Jaden, and a daughter, Jaz.

2. Mary Lou Retton

Mary Lou Retton vaulted to sporting superstar status during the 1984 Olympic games. The first American to win the women's all around gymnastics competition at the Olympics, Retton's five medals was the biggest haul by an athlete at the '84 games. Mary Lou and her husband Shannon Kelly have four daughters: Shayla, McKenna, Skyla, and Emma.

3. Marion Jones

Jones, the fastest women in the world and the 2000 Olympic 100 meter champion, has a son named Tim Montgomery. The boy is named after his father, Tim Montgomery, Jones' boyfriend and the world record holder in the men's 100 meter dash. No doubt that will be one tough kid to keep up with!   ❀

4. Chris Evert

One of the most successful and consistent players to ever step on the tennis court, this member of the Tennis Hall of Famer has three sons—Alexander, Nicholas, and Colton—with her husband, ex-Olympic skier Andy Mill.

5. Nancy Kerrigan

Kerrigan will forever be remembered for her unfortunate role in one of the strangest and most vile episodes in sporting history. After leaving the ice at the U.S. Olympic figure skating trials, she was attacked by a man wielding a metal implement. It turns out he was acting on behalf of Kerrigan's biggest rival, Tanya Harding. This unfortunate act has tended to overshadow Kerrigan's Olympic success—she won the silver medal. She and her husband Jerry Solomon have one son, Matthew.

❀   ❀

Quotable Mom

*"As my children grow older, I feel it's extremely important
to make them understand just how much Mommy loves her work.
I want them to realize that through hard work and a good
education, they, too, can become anything they choose.
I want my daughter to grow up respecting their working mom,*

to be proud of me and view me as their role model.
But that won't happen if they feel in anyway that
my career detracted from my role as their mother and
their biggest source of support and understanding—
and that's exactly why balancing your job and your
family is so incredibly important."
—*Mary Lou Retton,* I Love Being a Mom:
Treasured Stories, Memories and Milestones

Beautiful Moms

Take Five: Five Model Moms

1. Elle Macpherson

This Australian-born supermodel is best known for her multiple *Sports Illustrated* covers. She has appeared on the cover of that particular magazine a grand total of six times. One thing Macpherson didn't show on the covers of *SI* was her son Arpad!

2. Cindy Crawford

Named the world's highest paid supermodel in 1995 by no less an authority than *Forbes* magazine, Crawford was married for a brief time to actor Richard Gere. Crawford has two children with current husband Rande Gerber: a son named Presley and a daughter named Kaya.

3. Christie Brinkley

This Ford model superstar has appeared on over 500 magazine covers, as well as being the tempting love interest in *National Lampoon's Vacation*. Brinkley has three children: daughters Alexa Ray and Sailor Lee, and son Jack Paris.

4. Kate Moss

Kate Moss is generally credited with making emaciation chic! The waif-like Moss managed to eat for two, and has a beautiful baby boy named Jefferson for her efforts.

5. Rachel Hunter

This New Zealand born supermodel had two children—Renee and Liam—with her ex-husband, rocker Rod Stewart.

Mrs. America

There are roughly sixty million married women in the United States. Each year, the Mrs. America pageant elects one of them as the most poised, beautiful, and accomplished woman from fifty-one jurisdictions in the United States. The Mrs. America pageant began in 1977, and has steadily grown. In 1990, the pageant marked a milestone when its two-hour internationally-televised special broadcast became the first entertainment special to be produced in Moscow. The 2004 pageant was won by Mrs. Missouri, Heidi Dinan. In the 2004 contest, thirty-seven of the fifty-one contestants were mothers.

Brave Moms

Mom Fends Off Hungry Kitty!

Many moms have had to deal with their kids having a run-in with an animal, but not usually one this dangerous. In July 2001, six-year-old Nisha Devi was leaving her home in India's Chadyara village when she was attacked by a cat—a great big cat. A full-grown leopard had been hiding in the Devi's courtyard, and it figured young Nisha would make an easy meal.

The leopard pounced on Nisha and dragged her into a field.

Nisha's mother quickly raised the alarm and gave chase to the cat. The leopard soon realized that Nisha's mother wasn't going to let her daughter be an easy meal, and it dropped the little girl and ran off. Despite her all-too-close encounter with the big cat, Nisha is alive and doing well thanks to the courage and quick thinking of her mother.

Moms of Tiananmen

On June 4, 1989, the Chinese government cracked down on a group of protesters who had been occupying Tiananmen Square for over a month. Many student protesters were killed when the military opened fire, among them Jiang Jielian, a seventeen-year-old student. Jiang's death prompted his mother Ding Zilin to found Tiananmen Mothers' Organization, a group dedicated to uncovering the truth about what happened that deadly summer night.

For fifteen years, Ding has worked to gather information about the protesters and the government's actions against them. This hasn't been easy for Ding—over the course of her struggle she has lost her job as a university instructor, been kicked out of the Chinese Communist Party, and been detained by the Chinese government. Still, her steadfast dedication to her cause has made her a symbolic leader for many Chinese who want the government to account for its actions and reveal the truth behind what happened to the hundreds of protesters killed in Tiananmen Square.

Scientific Proof of What We All Know: Moms Are Courageous!

According to a scientific study, women with children are calmer and cooler under pressure than are childless women. In an experiment using rats, University of Richmond neuroscientist

Craig Kinsley discovered that rats that had given birth to one or more litters were less stressed when provoked than rats with no litters.

When Kinsley examined his subjects' brains, he found that the part of the brain that controlled fear showed much less activity among mother rats. Kinsley concluded that this is probably because mother rats have to protect their offspring, and if they are frozen by fear, they and their children may be eaten by predators.

Moreover, Kinsley discovered that mother rats also did better in a maze test than their childless cousins. This led Kinsley to conclude that not only are mother rats smarter than those who have no children, they are also calmer and braver. Said Kinsley, "There's something about pregnancy and subsequent exposure to offspring that create a more adaptive brain, one that's generally less susceptible to fear and stress." Although this study focused on rodents, the findings are likely true for humans as well, since humans and rats share many of the same genes, and such primal instincts are probably common.

A Mom's Brave Visit to Iraq

When the United States went to war in Iraq, Susan Galleymore's son Nick was among the troops sent overseas. While most moms would be worried about their child serving in a dangerous combat area, few would act on this fear in the same manner as Susan. Concerned about Nick's safety and living conditions in Iraq, Susan spoke with other military moms to find out what was going on in Iraq. She didn't find out much. Most moms were like her and had little information about what was happening there. Frustrated by this lack of information, Susan decided see for herself what was happening in Iraq! On January 24, 2004, Susan Galleymore took off to find her son, traveling over 7,400 miles from her home in Alameda to the deserts of Iraq.

Nick was worried about his mom's safety, and as late as three days before she set out had implored her not to come and refused to tell her where he was located. But this mom could not be stopped. Susan made the trip, and spent the first few days in Iraq visiting hospitals and orphanages to get a first-hand account of the horrors of war.

With his mom already "in country," Nick relented and told her where he was stationed. On February 1, 2004 she was at the gate of her son's base. When he saw his mom, Nick's face lit up. They only had a brief time together, but those precious minutes made the entire trip worthwhile. Said Galleymore of her trip, "I wouldn't change a thing, but I felt sad when I went home." No doubt she will feel happier again when Nick returns home from his tour in Iraq.

❀ Mom @ Home

Since the beginning of time, moms have had to know everything about everything. Moms have had many jobs in the home: master chef, seamstress, home nurse, psychologist, nutritionist, chauffeur, queen-of-clean, and the list goes on.

- It was not until the thirteenth century that the term "housewife" or "housework" came to be used.

- In agrarian pre-industrial America, moms and dads toiled side by side, at home and in the field, but mom was responsible for domestic chores, too.

The industrial revolution brought massive changes to mom's role. As men found work in factories, women were relegated to the home to care for the family.

- The same industrial revolution that created the "home" as mom's sphere also saw the birth of new technologies to help mom at home.
- Newfangled gadgets were invented to allow moms to do more, supposedly in less time.

Home is Where the Hearth Is

No other room in the house has demanded more time and energy of moms throughout history than the kitchen.

Medieval Kitchens

- Contained open hearths and a series of hooks, chains, and pulleys from which to hang cooking pots and kettles.
- Western Europeans did not use eating utensils until the sixteenth and seventeenth centuries. Sorry mother, we had to use our hands.
- The complexity of your kitchen reflected your social class.
- Medieval families lived off the land. After working for hours in

the field, moms would put in grueling hours in the kitchen, preparing food under less-than-ideal cooking conditions.

Early American Kitchens

In early American kitchens, moms were literally responsible for "keeping the home fires burning." They were always preparing for the next meal, for the next season, stretching meager home-grown resources as only mothers can do.

The kitchen was the "control center" of the whole house. Here, mom prepared food for market, dealt with bloody noses and scraped knees, washed and mended clothes, and prepared dinner. And, like today's kitchen, it was the site of family time, where families ate their meals and talked about their day.

Revolutionized Kitchens

The industrial revolution of the nineteenth century gave mom new tools to use in her kitchen. The cook stove was invented in the eighteenth century, quickly replacing the hearth. Stoves made it easier to keep a fire going, and provided more even and efficient heat.

Let's Heat Things Up

- In 1860, stoves cost a family from $5 to $25.

- Stoves were big business, and American families were purchasing them as quickly as they were being made. The 1860 Census of Manufacturers in America shows that 1 in 3 cast iron products being produced in the U.S. that year were stoves.

Canned Goods

- Napoleon himself is reported to have offered a prize to anyone who could develop a new method of preserving food so that he could more easily feed his army. Moms, as much as Napoleon's army, benefited from canned goods.

- Food stuffs from fruits and vegetables to meat could now be stored for long periods without spoiling.
- Canned goods also allowed busy moms with some disposable income to open cans of meat and vegetables, instead of spending hours preparing the same meal from scratch.

The More Things Change...

Gadgets might have made mom's work easier, but mom still carries much of the domestic workload, according to a survey by Baby Talk.

- On average, mom does forty hours of housework a week. Dad does just sixteen.
- According to a survey by Shell, 60 percent of moms say they do all or most household chores.
- Thirty-four percent of moms wish their husbands would help out more around the house
- It might be small consolation, but 64 percent of teens surveyed say that mom gets an "A" for how she runs the home.

Quotable Mom

"He taught me housekeeping; when I divorce I keep the house."
— Zsa Zsa Gabor

"Housework is what a woman does that nobody notices unless she hasn't done it." —Evan Esar

Behold: The Cookbook

- One of the first known cookbooks, a clay tablet from Babylon, dates back to circa 1500 BC.

- Until the eighteenth century, cookbooks were tools of the wealthy, and mistresses would read cookbooks aloud to their illiterate servants.

- In 1796 the first American cookbook, *American Cookery* by Amelia Simmons, was published. It was the first to include "American" ingredients like pumpkin, squash, and corn.

- In 1845, the first cookbook to give ingredients, quantities, and timing of recipes in a uniform manner was published.

- A century later, in 1896, Fannie Farmer perfected the recipe formula by using scientific measures in her cookbook, *Boston Cooking School Cook Book.*

- In 1931, one of the most enduring modern cookbooks hit kitchen counters across North America when *The Joy of Cooking* was published. The book, written by Irma Rumbauer, was a mother-daughter project. It was illustrated by Rumbauer's daughter, Marion.

Beat It!

Modern Americans take the eggbeater for granted. But when this gadget was invented in the nineteenth century, American moms were probably ecstatic. Most recipes of that time called for a lot of eggs—eggs that had to be beaten by hand. Consider this simple cake recipe from the early 1800s:

"Take eight eggs, yolks and whites, beat it for three quarters of an hour" —*The Frugal Housewife or Complete Woman Cook*, by Susannah Carter

Three quarters of an hour?

Even more daunting was the beating required in Mrs. Horace

Mann's 1861 *Christianity in the Kitchen* recipe for Angel Food Cake. It may have been heavenly, but the egg beating involved can only be described as hellish. This fluffy concoction required twenty eggs that had to be beaten for more than three hours!

- The first mechanical eggbeater was invented in 1884 by African-American Willis Johnston of Cincinnati.

- In 1885 beaters went electric when the first patent for an electric beater was issued to Rufus M. Eastman.

Baby Bites

In the summer of 1927, Dorothy Gerber was busily straining solid foods for her baby, Sally, on the advice of her pediatrician. Fed up with the tedious task, Dorothy suggested to her husband Daniel, owner of the Fremont Canning Company, that his company produce pureed entrees for babies. Daniel recognized his wife's idea for what it was—brilliant.

- By late 1928, after months of product testing courtesy of young Sally, strained peas, prunes, carrots, and spinach were ready to go on the market.

- The company launched a massive advertising campaign for its product, and within six months Gerber Baby Foods were on store shelves across the nation.

- Today Gerber offers two hundred different food choices and is sold in eighty countries around the world.

She Works Hard for No Money

According to the 1924–25 census, moms did an average of forty-eight to sixty-one hours of housework each week.

The 1940s

By 1940, most American homes were equipped with modern gadgets to help mom.

- Eighty percent were wired for electricity
- Seventy percent had electric irons
- Fifty-two percent had power washing machines
- Fifty-two percent had refrigerators
- Forty-seven percent had power vacuum cleaners
- Fifty-three percent had built-in bathing apparatus in their homes.

The Domestic Front

During WWII, Mom did much to support the war on the "domestic front." At home she managed her family, keeping them safe and happy while their dads were at war. She also observed rationing, grew a "Victory garden," made clothes to keep military men warm, and collected aluminum for munitions. And she often did double duty, embracing work outside the home in wartime factory production.

The 1950s

"There must be an individual touch to produce good meals."
—Silver Jubilee Super Market Cook Book, 1955

At war's end, women were encouraged to abandon jobs and return full-time to the home. Motherhood became mom's most important job and her life's work. Making dinner for her children and husband became an art form, and Betty Crocker was happy to show moms everywhere just how to do it.

Getting to the bottom of diapers

In the first three years of life, moms change a lot of diapers—as many as ten thousand! But if modern moms think they spend a lot of their lives changing their babies, imagine what life was like before disposables.

- In Elizabethan England, diapers were squares of cloth tied around baby's bottom with a string around the waist.

- No wonder sixteenth century England was so stinky—most babies got a fresh diaper just once every four days!

- On the American western frontier, moms made and washed all their baby diapers by hand. Given the workloads of frontier moms, wet diapers were seldom washed, but were allowed to dry by the fire before being reused.

- The first mass-produced all-cotton diapers were made in the United States dating from 1887. They were purchased as rectangles which mom (and big brothers and sisters) would have to fold.

- During World War II, diaper washing services sprang up all over the country, helping moms juggle baby care with their war-time factory work.

- The1950s saw the invention of pre-folded diapers, a huge time-saver for busy baby-boom moms.

- Marion Donovan revolutionized diapering in the mid 1950s when she cut up an old shower curtain to invent the "Boater," a plastic covering for cloth diapers. A year later Donovan fashioned the first pin-less "disposable" diaper. Initially Donovan could get no one to market her product, so she did it herself. A few years later, she sold her diaper company for $1 million.

- Early disposable diapers were "luxury" items, used just for special occasions.

- In 1961 Pampers launched their line of disposable pampers to an incredibly receptive audience.

TV Dinners

In 1954, C.A. Swanson & Sons introduced the first TV dinner. Marketed as a time-saver for moms and an innovation that made the most of the new TV culture of 1950s America, TV dinners were immediate hits.

- The first TV dinner was roast turkey with stuffing and gravy, sweet potatoes, and peas.

- Allegedly, a Swanson & Son executive came up with the idea as a way to use leftover Thanksgiving turkey.

- The idea of using aluminum trays was borrowed from airline practice of the day.

- The dinner sold for 98 cents.

- To this day, turkey dinners remain the most popular of the Swanson frozen dinner line-up (Swanson stopped calling them TV dinners in 1962).

- In 1986, microwavable trays replaced the aluminum, making for an even quicker dinner fix for busy modern moms.

- How famous are TV dinners? In 1999 Swanson received a star on the Hollywood walk of fame for its innovation.

Roundtable

Despite the busy times in which we live, isn't it nice to know dinner is still "family time"? In a survey of mothers by ClubMom, 62 percent reported that their family eats dinner together five or more nights a week.

Time Saving Devices?

According to a time-use data census conducted in 1965, American women were found to be doing, on average, about 7.5 hours of combined housework and child care each day.

Tupperware: For the Love of Leftovers

Where would we be without these handy plastic containers? In 1947 plastics innovator Earl Silas Tupper, an employee with the DuPont Chemical Company, patented his newly invented plastic containers. In experimenting with a piece of inflexible polyethylene slag, a waste product of the oil refining process, Tupper discovered that the substance could be molded into light-weight, air-tight, non-breakable containers.

- Originally, Tupper sold his containers in stores.

- When sales lagged, he pulled them off store shelves and began selling direct through home sales.

- Brownie Wise, a charismatic single mother, was one of his first direct sellers. It was under her direction that the Tupperware Party was born.

- Today, Tupperware sells $1.2 billion a year, worldwide.

- Every 2 seconds, someone, somewhere, buys a piece of Tupperware.

Did You Know…?

Dry baking mixes of all sorts originated in the industrial revolution. In 1947, the American company, Betty Crocker, began producing one of the first cake mixes, a ginger cake.

What a Crock

It may come as a surprise to many that Betty Crocker is not a real person. She began as a pen name in 1921, answering cooking-related questions posed to the company. Being fictitious has not held her back. Her portrait has been "painted" seven times over the past eight decades, the most recent marking Betty's seventy-fifth birthday. For someone who has spent her life in the kitchen, she hasn't aged a bit!

DOMESTIC DECADENCE: JULIA CHILD

Born Julia McWilliams in August 1912 to an upper-middle-class Pasadena, California family, Julia grew up with a family cook. She spent so little time in the kitchen that according to her biographer she could scarcely boil water when she graduated from Smith College.

During World War II, from 1941 to 1945, she worked in Ceylon (Sri Lanka) and China for the Office of Strategic Services (OSS, the forerunner of the CIA), where she met and married Paul Cushing Child. After the war Paul was assigned to the American embassy in Paris and in grand Paris Child began her culinary career at the premier French cooking school, Cordon Bleu. In 1961, the forty-nine-year-old Child published her first of what would be many cookbooks, to rave reviews.

This book led to the debut of Child's PBS show *The French Chef*. Child's strongest asset was her personality—she was funny, opinionated, and very human. She worked tirelessly to show other women how much fun and creative cooking could be. In all she starred in eight television series and published more than ten books. "Dining with one's friends and beloved family is certainly one of life's primal and most innocent delights, one that is both soul-satisfying and eternal," she remarked in the introduction to her seventh book, *The Way to Cook*. Child died in August 2004, two days before her ninety-second birthday.

Did You Know...?

Julia Child's kitchen is now preserved as an exhibit at the Smithsonian Institution in Washington.

ERMA BOMBECK

While Julia was in the kitchen teaching moms how to enjoy their cooking, Erma Bombeck, a Dayton, Ohio humorist, was helping moms to laugh at themselves. Born in Dayton in 1927, Bombeck grew up in poverty. At age twenty she was given devastating news that an inherited kidney disease would lead inevitably to kidney failure. She went on with her life, determined not be controlled by her disease.

Although told by her university teachers that she would never realize her dream of becoming a journalist, Erma showed the same tenacity with which she faced her illness, and in 1949 became a journalist with an Ohio paper. That same year she married Bill Bombeck. After raising three children in the 1950s and '60s, Bombeck returned to journalism, this time with a daily humor column, "At Wit's End."

For the next thirty years Bombeck found the humor in being a woman, a mother, and a housewife. In 1991, Bombeck was diagnosed with breast cancer and in 1993, the anticipated kidney failure struck. In April 1996 Bombeck received a kidney transplant, but died a few days later. During her career she published more than four-thousand columns in nine-hundred newspapers across America and wrote more than fifteen bestselling books.

Quotable Mom

"When it comes to cooking, five years ago I felt guilty 'just adding water.' Now I want to bang the tube against the countertop and have a five-course meal pop out. If it comes with plastic silverware and a plate that self-destructs, all the better." —Erma Bombeck

"Housework can't kill you, but why take a chance?"
—Phyllis Diller

"I do not refer to myself as a 'housewife'
for the reason that I did not marry a house."
—Wilma Scott Heide

"By and large, mothers and housewives are the only workers who
do not have regular time off. They are the great vacationless class."
—Anne Morrow Lindbergh

Baking: A Lost Art?

- Seventy-one percent of Americans learned to cook from mom, according to a *Better Homes and Gardens* study.

- Eighty percent of kids said that mom has been teaching them how to cook. Only 29 percent reported that dad has been teaching them.

- Fifty percent of women say they enjoy cooking.

- When asked the main reason why that they like to cook at home, women were almost three times more likely than men to say that they like to cook at home because it is for their family.

High Praise

- A survey by Epicurious says mom is a great cook. Forty-six percent of Americans rate her cooking as almost as good as a professional.

- Nineteen percent said she'd win if they had to compete against her in an Iron Chef challenge.

Quotable Mom

*"Just think of all those women on the Titanic who said,
'No, thank you,' to dessert that night. And for what!"*
—Erma Bombeck

Warm Feelings

According to a ClubMom survey, working moms respect the
work of stay-at-home moms, and vice versa.

- Eighty percent of working mothers say they respect moms who
  work at home.

- Sixty-six percent of at-home mothers respect working mothers.

Don't Go There

Only 11 percent of moms surveyed by Proflowers, Inc. said they
would like to receive a kitchen appliance as a gift for Mother's Day.

Quotable Mom

*"The best time for planning a book is while
you're doing the dishes."*
❀   *—Agatha Christie*

*"There are practical little things in housekeeping
which no man really understands."*
—Eleanor Roosevelt

A Walk Thru Time

1490

The first stove, made entirely of brick and tile, is made in Alsace, France. (Modern cast iron stoves don't appear until the early eighteenth century, and they're a hit.)

1795

First patent for a corkscrew appears in England.

1797

The good ol' scrub board appears to help Mom get those whites their whitest. (The first mechanical drum washing machines don't appear for another fifty years.)

1805

American Oliver Evans manufactures the first artificial refrigeration machine. It doesn't catch on until the beginning of the twentieth century.

1850

Joel Houghton patents the first dishwasher in America: a hand-turned wheel that splashes water on dishes.

1858

John Mason patents the screw neck bottle or the "Mason Jar," which becomes a staple of the wide-spread canning going on in America at the time.

1882

New Yorker Henry W. Seely patents the first electric iron in America. (Steam irons don't appear until the 1950s.)

1884

Willis Johnson of Cincinnati introduces the first mechanical egg-beater to the American public.

1891

The first electric stoves appear in North America.

1893

Thomas Stewart patents the first clamping mop that could wring the water out of itself by the use of a lever.

1897

African-American Lloyd Ray patents the first dustpan.

1907

Scott Paper introduces the first paper towels. Originally they're intended solely for use in Philadelphia classrooms to help prevent the spread of the common cold from child to child.

1910

The first handheld motorized vacuum cleaners appear, sold by the Hoover Company.

1919

The modern pop-up timer toaster is introduced by American Charles Strite. Seems he got a little frustrated with the burnt toast always being served in the cafeteria at the manufacturing plant where he worked.

1922

Stephen Poplawski invents the blender, after putting a spinning blade at the top of a container. He uses it to mix fountain drinks. (Already popular in the medical field, it becomes popular among consumers in the 1950s.)

1930

General Electric markets the first electric kettle with an automatic cut-out.

1938

Nescafe, or freeze-dried "just add water" instant coffee, is introduced to the world.

1946

Self-taught engineer Percy Spencer discovers low-density microwave energy while experimenting with a new vacuum tube called a magnetron. He discovers the energy omitted can be contained in a box, and can raise the temperature of food. The microwave oven is born.

1950

Harry Wasylyk, a Canadian inventor from Winnipeg, Manitoba, introduces a new garbage bag made from disposable green polyethylene (plastic). They are first marketed in the 1960s as Glad Garbage bags. The first telephone answering machine, created by Bell Laboratories and Western Electric, also appears this year.

1953

Dow Chemical Company introduces thin sheets of clingy plastic for use at home in preserving food. They call it Saran Wrap.

1954

C.A. Swanson & Sons introduces the first TV dinner, consisting of roast turkey with stuffing and gravy, sweet potatoes, and peas.

1965

The first tabletop microwave ovens begin to appear, with the first home model priced at $1,295.

1971

Rival introduces the first Crock-Pot slow cooker, which opens up a whole new range of cooking ideas for the kitchen. It means mom can cook all day without having to be around and worrying that the food will burn.

1975

Sales of microwave ovens for the first time exceed those of gas ranges. Despite the new-found craze for gourmet cooking, the American public still wants convenience, too.

1980

Polyethylene Terephthalate (plastic) bottles really begin to catch on, and are suddenly widely used in food packaging. Before this, plastic packaging was mostly reserved for military use. Manufacturers begin to focus on ingenious packaging as marketing techniques for their products.

1990

Gourmet cooking is soon the craze, and the tools to help are popping up everywhere. Garlic presses, pepper mills, and cheese cutters are used like never before. Many previously unheard of tools are appearing in American kitchens everywhere.

2000

Luxury items are no longer luxury: wine chillers and home crepe makers find their way into more and more kitchens, and cuisine from around the world becomes commonplace in many American homes. Convenience is still part of the rage, though, with microwave ovens in over 90 percent of American kitchens now.

Baby's Bottle

All moms have to, at some point, feed their babies. Although nature is very accommodating, mom can't always provide the nourishment baby needs. For centuries, humankind has produced baby bottles.

- Efforts to simulate mother's breast milk go back to 2,000 BC.

- The earliest known "feeding cup," which resembled a decorated teapot, was discovered in Phoenikas, Cyprus, and is currently housed in the British Museum.

- Pottery was used for baby bottles right up until 250 BC, when the Egyptians invented blown glass.

- Europeans, however, did not catch on to glass until the middle of the nineteenth century. Up to that point, baby bottles were made from all kinds of materials, and fashioned into a variety of shapes, some looking like oil lamps, others like miniature wine jugs.

- Cow and goat horns were also common vessels and were topped with dried animal teats.

What Victoria Would Have Used

- If mother's milk was not available, Victorian children might be fed "pap," a soft gruel of cornmeal and crushed walnuts, which was blown into a baby's mouth.

- Bottles came in different shapes and sizes, made of glass and pewter. The most popular were shaped like a banjo, containing a glass and rubber tube system which allowed children to feed unattended.

- Because of the germs bred in these hard-to-clean vessels, brand names like "The Empire" or "Mummy's Darling" were disturbingly nicknamed "The Killer" or "The Murderer."

Nipple News

- Before the invention of rubber nipples, artificial nipples were often made from rags, chamois, sponge, wood, or dried animal teats, which were fitted over the end of bottles.

- The first rubber nipple appeared in 1845, designed by New Yorker Elijah Pratt.

- Early versions often contained lead, causing health concerns and a bad taste.

- By 1900, rubber was drastically improved and nipples caught on. Rubber would also be incorporated into pacifiers, which emerged in the early twentieth century.

Modern Glass Bottles

- The first glass baby bottle was patented in 1841 by Charles Windship. It was superimposed over a mother's breast, in order to convince the baby that it was actually drinking mother's milk.

- By the late nineteenth century, bottle makers sought to create safer products. The first modern glass bottle, which was shaped like a banana, appeared in 1880.

- Invented in 1910, the banana-shaped Allenbury Feeder would become the norm, remaining unchanged for about 50 years.

- By the end of World War II, 230 patents for baby bottles had been issued by the U.S. Patent Office.

- As time passed, cylindrical bottles gained acceptance primarily because they were easier to fit into mechanical sterilizers.

- While the merits of breast milk are widely acknowledged and while society increasingly enables women the ability to breastfeed, baby bottles remain a staple in the homes of all new parents.

The School Lunch

Every mom knows she cannot control her kids when they are not under her watchful eye. When it comes to the school cafeteria, mom certainly has no illusions.

- Sixty-nine percent of moms admitted that they suspect their kids are trashing the brown-bag lunch they packed for them that morning, according to an Oscar Mayer and KRC Research survey.

- Seventy-three percent of kids actually admit to doing so.

- Mom packs 73 percent of school lunches.

- Fifty-two percent of moms say that their biggest challenge in packing a school lunch is to make one that is nutritious and kid-approved.

- Forty-six percent of those lunches contain a deli-meat sandwich.

- Thirty percent are plain ol' peanut butter and jelly sandwiches.

- Forty percent of kids say they would rather buy their lunch at school.

Getting 'Round

Automobiles changed the family's home routine, and especially that of moms. By 1930, there were 36 million households in America, and 26 million registered automobiles. Women very quickly took up driving, and began to replace men as the primary providers of the household's transportation.

Today, minivans top the list of the best-selling vehicles in North America, year after year. It's no wonder. Between taking the kids to school, soccer practice, haircuts, grocery shopping, family road-trips, and PTA meetings, moms need practical vehicles to get them where they are going.

A Chance to Talk

According to a survey by Harris Interactive and Chrysler, 56 percent of parents feel they are always on the go.

- Nearly 70 percent say that most of the time they spend with their children outside of the home is in the family vehicle.

- On average, parents spend about 1.3 hours a day in the car.

- They take an average of 5.3 road trips per year.

- But this isn't necessarily a bad thing, since two thirds of parents say the family vehicle is one of the best places to communicate with their children.

- Ninety-one percent say they use time on the road to talk to their children about school.

- Ninety percent talk with them about their friends.

- Eighty-one percent talk to their children about lifestyle values during this time.

- Sixty-nine percent use the time to talk about chores.

- Sixty-five percent talk to their kids about issues such as drugs, alcohol, or sex, while driving around.

- Moms of school-aged children spend, on average, 74 minutes of their day driving together.

- Back in 1995 they only spent 67 minutes on the road.

- Moms of young kids spend 64 minutes on the road each day.

Tools of the Trade

Washing Machine

In the beginning, mom had to pound clothes on rocks and wash them in local streams. The first real "washing machine" was the scrub board, which appeared in 1797, powered, of course, by mom herself. After boiling clothes on the stove, or giving them a good rinse, mom would scrub away, often until her knuckles bled.

Thankfully, in 1851, American James King patented the first washing machine, a contraption with an internal drum that spun the clothes. Though it was hand powered, it was much less tiring than the old scrub board. The first electric washing machines were manufactured in 1908 by the Hurley Machine Company of Chicago. They were a galvanized tub with an electric motor. Only a year earlier, the Maytag Corporation went into the washing machine business, after a slow year of selling farm equipment.

Stove

It was not until the early eighteenth century that cast iron stoves became popular in Britain and America and began to replace the open hearth. The first stoves were a cast iron box. Soon folks started cooking on the top, putting holes in the top for pots to sit in.

Suddenly moms were able to cook, bake, and do laundry, all over the same fire. In 1826 the first gas powered stove was introduced, and by 1833 the first coal powered stove appeared. In 1891, the first electric stove appeared, and became wide-spread in affluent homes across America throughout the 1920s and 30s.

Almost Too Good to be True: Self-Cleaning Oven

Picture it: Back-breaking stretching. Shoulder-killing scrubbing. Choking, noxious fumes. Cleaning ovens the "old fashioned way" was no picnic. In 1982, this all changed with the patenting of the first self-cleaning oven. How does this modern miracle work? These marvels of modern technology use a 900-degree Fahrenheit temperature cycle to burn off spills, with no need for chemical cleaners. A special lock ensures the oven door stays closed to prevent injury while it works its magic.

Electric Iron

The iron itself has been around for centuries, often simply a warm brick or rock used to smooth out clothing. In 1882, Henry W. Seeley, a New York inventor, patented his "electric flatiron." The first electric iron was no featherweight, topping the scales at almost fifteen pounds. By modern standards it was not particularly efficient, but for moms who previously had to heat cast irons on open fires with no temperature consistency, Seeley's electric flatiron was a vast improvement.

Quotable Mom

*"My second favorite household chore is ironing.
My first being hitting my head on the top bunk bed until I faint."*
—*Erma Bombeck*

Dishwasher

In 1886, Madge and her hand-softening Palmolive were nowhere to be found. Josephine Cochran of Shelbyville, Illinois, probably up to her wrinkled hands in dishwater, resolved: "If nobody else is going to invent a dishwashing machine, I'll do it myself." And she did.

- Cochrane unveiled the first working automatic dishwashing machine at the World's Fair in Illinois in 1893.

- Her prototype dishwasher was a wooden tub with a wire basket inside; the dishes were placed in the basket and rollers rotated them. As a handle on the tub was turned, hot, soapy water was sprayed into the tub, washing the dishes.

- Though restaurants and hotels bought Cochran's machines, they were slow to catch on elsewhere. The public did not really embrace the dishwasher until the 1960s.

Toaster

The idea of eating burnt bread has been around for a while: it was common even to the ancient Romans who toasted bread mainly to prolong its life.

The word "toast" comes from the Latin "tostum," which means to burn, or scorch. The first toaster was invented in 1893 by Crompton & Co. in Britain and introduced in the United States in 1909. The first toasters cooked one side of the bread at a time and you needed to flip it manually. In 1919, American inventor Charles Strite invented the modern pop-up timer toaster.

What Makes Toast Tasty?

- Thirty-eight percent of Americans like their toast simply buttered.

- Two percent favor jam or jelly.
- Thirteen percent like peanut butter.
- Eight percent like cheese on their toast.
- Six percent like Nutella.

Vacuum Cleaner

Before 1900, most carpets were cleaned rather ineffectively by beating them with a broom. By the turn of the century, the first mechanized carpet cleaning systems was devised, consisting of a rather inefficient system of horse drawn vacuums.

The first handheld vacuums appeared around 1910. The first vacuum cleaner, invented by a janitor in Ohio, consisted of an old fan motor attached to a soap box and stapled to a broom handle. A pillow case served as a dust collector. One of the first buyers of his patent was a cousin, whose husband, William H. Hoover, later became president of the Hoover Company.

Quotable Mom

"Nature abhors a vacuum. And so do I."
—Anne Gibbons

Clothes Dryer

The first clothes dryer was, of course, the wind. But you could not always count on it being around. In the early 1880s, enterprising Frenchmen developed an alternative to Mother Nature with a rudimentary dryer that was a simple barrel-shaped metal drum with holes in the side. Clothes would be placed in the rotating drum above a fire. In 1892, George T. Sampson got one of the first American patents for a clothes dryer, and by 1915 electric dryers made their appearance in moms' laundry rooms.

Microwave Oven

In 1946, engineer Percy Spender was testing a new vacuum tube called a magnetron. On completing his tests, he noticed that the candy bar in his pocket had melted. Further tests showed that the magnetron produced low-density microwave energy with heating capacity.

To harness this effect, Spencer fashioned a metal box with an opening into which he fed microwave power. Inside the box, the energy was contained, and could quickly raise the temperature of any food placed inside.

- The first commercial microwave oven appeared in 1946.

- It stood about 5.2 feet tall, and weighed over 750 pounds.

- Initially, fears about the ill effects of radiation and the potential health hazards prevented their wholesale acceptance.

- By the mid 1970s these fears had abated. Cooking was forever changed.

Quotable Mom

"It is ludicrous to read the microwave direction on the boxes of food you buy, as each one will have a disclaimer: 'THIS WILL VARY WITH YOUR MICROWAVE.' Loosely translated, this means, 'You're on your own, Bernice.'"
—Erma Bombeck

Refrigerator

Perhaps no other kitchen appliance has made mom's life easier. Originally mothers stored food in a cold cellar, in the ground, or even in well water. By the nineteenth century, block houses containing blocks of ice insulated in sawdust helped keep things cool, at least part of the year.

In 1805, American Oliver Evans invented the first means of artificial refrigeration. Early fridges used toxic gases such as ammonia and methyl chloride as refrigerants, but that, of course, has changed. Today, refrigerators appear in 99 percent of American homes.

Hint Hint Hint

One of the most endearing American personalities of the last forty years is the know-everything household guru, Heloise. The "Hints from Heloise" empire was started in 1958 when Heloise Cruse began a column in the *Honolulu Advertiser*. When Cruse passed away in 1977, her daughter, Ponce Kiah Marchelle Heloise Cruse, assumed her mother's name and legacy and continued the dynasty to this day. Her daily column appears in more than five-hundred newspapers around the world.

Quotable Mom

"I'm not a fanatical housekeeper like most people may think. My philosophy is always to pick up the big chunks and keep things neat. No one is going to look inside your oven, heaven forbid! If they do, they deserve what they find!"
—Heloise

Take Five: Top Five Hints from Heloise

1. To clean cloudy drinking glasses?

Heloise advises soaking them for an hour or more in warm (but not boiled) vinegar. Then use a nylon or plastic scrubber to remove the film. If the film remains, the damage must be etching, and is permanent.

2. To get rid of perspiration/deodorant stains on underarms of washable shirts?

Sponge on white vinegar or soak the garment in it, and wait thirty minutes. Launder shirts in the hottest water safe for the fabric.

3. To freshen the garbage disposal?

Sprinkle it with baking soda and a few drops of dishwashing liquid, and scrub well with a brush (a new toilet brush works great!). Turn on water and let the disposal flush thoroughly. Freshen with a citrus scent by running a few cut-up limes or lemon through the system, using lots of water.

4. To lift candle wax dripped onto carpet?

Once the wax hardens, scrape up what you can with a dull knife. Place paper towels or an old white cloth over the area and iron it on low-warm (no steam), pressing gently. Repeat until wax is lifted, and remove any stains with a spot remover or carpet cleaner.

5. To solve a roach problem?

Combine equal parts boric acid and sugar. Mix well. Sprinkle in crevices and, if building or remodeling, between walls before putting up plaster board. Put powder in jar lids and place behind fridge and under sinks. Caution: keep mixture away from pets and children. If ingested, boric acid can be harmful.

Quotable Mom

"Housework is a treadmill from futility to oblivion with stop-offs at tedium and counter productivity."
—Erma Bombeck

"I think housework is the reason most women go to the office."
—Heloise Cruse

*"Education is so important when it comes to domesticity.
I don't know why no one ever thought to paste a label on the toilet
tissue spindle giving 1-2-3 directions for replacing the tissue on it.
Then everyone in the house would know what Mama knows."*
—Erma Bombeck

16

Mythological Mom

The world has always been an unpredictable place. Ancient people had a yearning much like our own to understand the world and their place in it. That quest has produced beautifully creative mythologies and folklore. In these mythologies and folklore, motherhood has played a pivotal role.

These stories have helped shape the face of cultures the world over. As inheritors of these stories, to hear them is to hear our own story. To understand the mythological stories about motherhood is to comprehend ourselves and our understanding of motherhood.

To that end, the following are some of the more familiar and noteworthy of mothers in mythology. From the ancient Greeks and Romans, to the ancient Egyptians, to Hinduism and Buddhism, they provide insight into the qualities of motherhood honored in different cultures throughout history.

Greece

Mother Earth, Rhea, and Hera

According to Greek Mythology, Mother Earth emerged from Chaos as the universe formed. As she slept, she bore a son named Uranus who, with her, formed the face of the earth. She made the grass and flowers and trees, and the beasts and birds, while Uranus made the rivers and the waters flow.

Notable characters from Greek mythology were claimed to be descended from her, including the Cyclopes and Odysseus. It is Uranus, however, who makes the headlines by fathering, with Mother Earth, the first set of Greek gods, the Titans. Having killed his rebellious sons, the Cyclopes, Mother Earth was enraged and persuaded her Titan children to attack their father. Led by Cronus, the youngest of the seven Titans, they surprised Uranus as he slept and castrated him.

Cronus was soon crowned king of the gods, and married his sister Rhea. They produced a number of children, but Cronus swallowed all of them fearing a prophecy from his parents which stated that one of his own sons would dethrone him. Rhea, as any mom would be, was outraged, and upon bearing their third son, named Zeus, stole him away in the dead of night to Mount Lycaeum and gave him to Mother Earth. When Rhea came back to Cronus on Mount Olympus, she handed her husband a stone she had wrapped in swaddling clothes, which he promptly swallowed. Cronus soon found out the deception, and Zeus and Cronus warred for ten years.

Again, Mother Earth intervened, and prophesied victory to her grandson, Zeus, if he took up as allies those whom Cronus had turned away. Ever a dutiful son, Zeus quickly met up with the Cyclopes, who gave him a thunderbolt as a weapon of defense, Hades, who gave him a helmet, and Poseidon who gave him a trident. Defeat was swift, and Zeus overthrew the old Titan gods, establishing the new order of Olympian gods, with Zeus as their king.

Zeus soon took his sister Hera as his wife, and she ruled as queen of the gods and goddess of marriage. In some versions of the story, she conceived all of her children alone, after beating her hand on the ground or eating lettuce. Being mother of the gods couldn't have been easy, with Zeus always running around and having affairs with other women. In fact, she spent most of her time plotting revenge on those women with whom her husband was consorting.

Aphrodite

Aphrodite was born from the sea foam that formed after Cronus cut off Uranus' genitals and his bodily fluids dropped into the sea. As the goddess of love, sex, and beauty, her connection to motherhood is somewhat obvious. She was also the mother of Aeneas, who fought in the Trojan War, and was a hero in the later establishment of Rome.

Jocasta

Sigmund Freud talked a lot about her son, Oedipus, but don't forget that it takes two to tango. Jocasta was the famed Queen of Thebes, married to Lauis. According to prophecy, their child was destined to kill its father, so Jocasta took her newborn son up into the mountains and left him there to die.

He was found by a kind shepherd who named the child Oedipus and gave him to King Polybus of Corinth. When Oedipus grew up, he found out about the prophecy, and being a good son, promptly left Corinth as to avoid killing his father. Along the way he ran into a bandit, and not knowing the man was his biological father, ended up killing King Laius anyway. Time passed and he arrived in Thebes, where he won Queen

Jocasta as a prize for killing a monster. The two unknowingly married and had four children together. No happily ever after here, though; Jocasta, upon finding out the truth, took her own life.

Rome

Ceres: What A Mother's Love Can Accomplish

When Rome was founded, its mythology wasn't yet complex. Roman gods were just "numina," or faceless, formless forces. It wasn't until the Romans encountered Greek culture that their own mythology began to form, often with very strong parallels.

Ceres is a great example of that. She was the daughter of Saturn and Rhea (known by the Greeks as Cronus and Rhea, respectively). Her brother was Jupiter (or Zeus, to the Greeks) and she must have been really fond of him because she bore a daughter named Proserpine with him. It was believed that the joy Ceres felt every year upon being reunited with her daughter caused the earth to bring forth fruits and grains. She came to be associated as the goddess of grain and growing plants, and the goddess of love that a mother bears for her child.

Queen Juno

While Ceres may have been the goddess of fertility, the real mother of the gods was Juno. She was married to Jupiter, and together they ruled as King and Queen. As the goddess of heaven and the moon, she symbolized the qualities desired of a Roman woman. She was a warrior and protector of Rome, often appearing armed and wearing a goatskin cloak. She was also believed to protect women during childbirth, rearing, and during their preparation for marriage. It was believed that she was present during all marriage ceremonies.

Venus

The daughter of Jupiter and Dione, Venus was regarded as the goddess of love and the "queen of pleasure," not to mention the mother of the Roman people. This mom got around, having amorous romps with many men, including Mars, Adonis, and Anchises, the father of Aeneas. She also bore a son, named Cupid, who became the god of love. With all that, it's not hard to imagine why she became known as the bringer of joy to the gods and humans.

Hinduism & Buddhism

Devi

In Hindu mythology, Devi is the Divine Mother of Hindu culture. Her name itself means "goddess," and she can appear in many forms, whether as a warrior, consort, wife, and, of course, mother. As the wife of Shiva, the god of generation and destruction, Devi holds joy and pain in her right hand, and life and death in her left hand. She brings rain and protects against disease, making her the goddess of nature. As a mother of life, she is the goddess of creative power and represents all women in the universe. She is, however, also the mother of death, and can appear as a bloodthirsty warrior, fighting against evil. And moms take heed, according to Hindu tradition, Devi is present in all women's souls.

Momma Maya

You're fast asleep one night and you suddenly dream of a child being placed in your womb in the shape of a little white elephant. What do you do? In the sixth century BC, an Indian Queen named Maya experienced this as a sign of the birth of a world savior. When the time came for the child to be born, she went to a grove where the child emerged from her right side without having caused her any pain. The child was Buddha, who was immediately endowed with the power of speech. He would go on to found the Buddhist religion, and his mother would die only seven days after his birth because of the joy his birth caused her.

Ancient Egypt

From the Neith

For Ancient Egyptians, you can't get much higher up the mother goddess scale than Neith. She was believed to have emerged from the primeval water to create the world. Following the course of the Nile to the sea, she formed the city of Salis upon reaching the Delta. She was considered the goddess who first created the seeds of gods and men.

Often considered to be the mother of Egyptian rulers, she also bore Ra, the sun god, considered the creator and controller of the universe, and one of the most worshiped of Egyptian gods. It was believed that the deceased could receive her divine power by means of the mummy's wrappings, as those bandages were often considered the gifts of Neith.

Isis

Originally the goddess of royalty, this deity decided to expand her realm, and eventually became known as the goddess of motherhood and fertility in ancient Egypt. She was the by-product of the goddess of the sky and the god of the earth. She married her brother Osiris, and bore a son named Horus, who was often the god associated with the living king. But when it came to being symbolized in Egyptian culture, well, we've got to say that it wasn't all that flattering, especially for a mother. Usually she was symbolized by a cow or a cow's head or horns. In art she was often depicted with her son, Horus, along with a crown and a vulture.

Australian Aboriginal

Australian Aborigines are thought to have the oldest maintained cultural history on earth, spanning some 50,000 years or more. The central unifying theme of their mythology and folklore is that all life as we know it today is part of a vast and complex network of relationships, which can be traced back directly to the great spirit ancestors, or "dreamtime".

When it comes to creation, they believe that the creator goddess Eingana, a snake goddess who lives in dreamtime, is the mother of all water, animals, and humanity. She holds a sinew that is attached to all living things, and if she let's go, an organism will die. She has no vagina, and simply grew in size, unable to give birth to the life growing inside of her. In order to give birth to the universe, she had to have the god Barraiya open a hole with a spear near her anus.

Babylon, Syria, and Sumeria

Ishtar: An Earthy Kind of Gal

Throughout the ancient pagan Mediterranean world, especially in Babylonia, there were numerous cultures and societies that worshipped a mother goddess of fertility, often known as Ishtar. She was often known by different names to different cultures. In Syrian and Palestinian, the Phoenicians called her Astarte, while in Phyrgia and Lydia she was known as Cybele. In Sumeria, where the cult of the mother goddess probably originated, she was called Inanna or Innina.

Throughout, her story was generally the same. In the spring, she and her young lover would have a passionate affair, after which she would drive him mad. This would allow her to give birth to the renewal of the earth in the spring. The young lover would then, in his madness, castrate himself and die, but return annually to do it all over again. When it came to worshipping this mother goddess, the rites were often designed to increase human fertility.

Celtic

Danu, Danu

While there doesn't seem to be any surviving creation story within Irish mythology, the Irish Celts aren't without their mythological moms. The most famous is Danu, considered to be the mother of all the Celtic gods, and especially the mother goddess of the Tribes of Danu, who are believed to have been amongst the original clans that settled in Ireland around the first century BC, and were the origin of the Celtic peoples.

They were a people believed to have originated from around the Danube River, aptly named after their mother goddess, and eventually making Danu a river goddess. Celtic history often recounts stories of battles between the Celts and the Fomorians, who worshipped a mother goddess named Domnu.

As Celtic mythology emerged, numerous battles ensued between the Children of Domnu, representing darkness, and the Children of Danu, representing light and order, making it a battle symbolic of the fight between good and evil, which they consider to still rage on even today. Danu also briefly appears in Hindu mythology as the primordial goddess of waters, present at the creation of the world.

Brigid

The traditional matron of healing, medicine, and fertility, Brigid is also the goddess who presides over the cradle of a newborn infant for the Celts. It is not uncommon for Celtic women to hand crosses over their cradles while praying to Brigid for protection for their child. As Christianity spread to Ireland, though,

Brigid came to be known as a foster mother to Jesus, present as a midwife to the Virgin Mary at the birth of Christ, even if the Bible had overlooked her presence somehow. In Welsh folklore, Brigid is known as Ceridwen, who is said to have been the mother of the famous Welsh poet, Taliesin.

Norse

Frigga

In Norse mythology, Frigga was the wife of Odin, the father of the Norse gods, making her the mother goddess. Also a goddess of love, fertility, marriage, and destiny, she spun the thread of time, carrying with her the knowledge of eternity, though she never revealed it to anyone.

It is her love for her son that makes her a notable mythological mom. According to legend, when her son Baldur was born she made every tree, plant, and animal promise not to harm her son, but in her haste she forgot to acquire the consent of the mistletoe. It was Loki, a mischievous Norse god, who caught this oversight, and tricked another of the Norse gods into fashioning a spear out of a branch of mistletoe, using it to kill Baldur.

Baldur's death brought about winter to the world, and every spring it is said that the Norse gods have resurrected Baldur, bringing an end to the winter weather. In commemoration of her son's resurrection, Frigga appointed mistletoe a sacred plant of peace, so as to avoid it being characterized as a plant of death. With this designation, when two people walk under mistletoe they are required to give each other a kiss of peace.

Eastre...or Easter

This nature goddess Eastre was often associated with overseeing the rebirth of nature in the spring after the long, cold winter. She also gradually came to be considered the goddess responsible for eggs, making her an obvious choice as a mother goddess. By some accounts, it is claimed that as Scandinavia began to be Christianized, many of the early Christian Northmen refused to abandon the festival in early spring celebrating Eastre.

Gradually the festival honoring this goddess came to be combined with the story of the resurrection of Jesus Christ, in order to expedite the process of Christianizing the Northmen. The name of Easter survives as a Christian holiday to this day.

Wicca

Great Mother Goddess

While Wiccans maintain that they don't worship any god in particular, all Wiccans do generally agree that they worship the great Mother Goddess and her male consort, the Horned God. For them, the great Mother Goddess has been known throughout history, just under many different names: Aphrodite, Brigit, Ceres, Cerridwen, Demeter, Isis, Venus, and so on.

For Wiccans, the great Mom in the sky isn't a "someone," but a "something" with powerful forces or energy that can be harnessed and directed through human intervention. The gods and goddesses are symbols of the life forces and processes of the world, and all the myths, legends and metaphors throughout history have been an attempt to explain what they are.

Modern Wiccan spirituality is based on the works of Gerald Gardner in the late 1950s. Given all this, Wiccan spirituality is often a mixture of ancient Greek, Roman, pagan, or Celtic practices and beliefs, making the Mother Goddess of Wicca a woman of many forms and personalities.

Africa

Mawu

An African goddess for the Fon people in the Dahomey Region of West Africa, in the Republic of Benin, Mawu is considered a great creator mother goddess, and the goddess of motherhood, joy, and the night. With her partner, Liza, she created the world.

According to legend, after creating the earth and all life on it, she asked Awe, a monkey she had created to help out by making some more animals out of clay. The monkey soon became arrogant, however, and climbed up into the heavens to show Mawu that he too could give life.

Awe failed, however, after Mawu made him a poisonous bowl of porridge to remind him that only she could give life, and that she could also take it away. Seeing all this chaos caused Gbadu, the first woman that Mawu had created, to send her own daughter Minona out among the people and remind them that only Mawu can give the breath of life.

Ala

The Ibo people of Nigeria worship an earth mother goddess of fertility and death named Ala, above all. Begotten by the Sun God, Chuku, she is often depicted with a small child in her arms. According to these legends, this mom gives birth to all of humanity, and the souls of the dead reside in her womb, awaiting rebirth once more.

A Note to My Amazing Mom